MOMENTS WITH GOD

for

Grandparents

100 DEVOTIONS TO
CONNECT FAITH AND FAMILY

Our Daily Bread
Publishing™

Moments with God for Grandparents: 100 Devotions to Connect Faith and Family
© 2023 by Our Daily Bread Ministries

Requests for permission to quote from this book should be directed to: Permissions Department, Our Daily Bread Publishing, PO Box 3566, Grand Rapids, MI 49501, or contact us by email at permissionsdept@odb.org.

The devotional readings collected in this book were previously published over a span of years in *Our Daily Bread* devotional booklets that are distributed around the world in more than fifty languages.

Scripture quotations, unless otherwise indicated, are taken from the Holy Bible, New International Version®, NIV®. Copyright © 1973, 1978, 1984, 2011 by Biblica, Inc.™ Used by permission of Zondervan. All rights reserved worldwide. www.zondervan.com.

Scripture quotations marked NKJV are taken from the New King James Version®. Copyright © 1982 by Thomas Nelson. Used by permission. All rights reserved.

Scripture quotations marked NLT are taken from the Holy Bible, New Living Translation, copyright © 1996, 2004, 2015 by Tyndale House Foundation. Used by permission of Tyndale House Publishers, Inc., Carol Stream, Illinois 60188. All rights reserved.

Interior design by Michael J. Williams

ISBN: 978-1-64070-258-5

Library of Congress Cataloging-in-Publication Data Available

Printed in China
23 24 25 26 27 28 29 30 / 8 7 6 5 4 3 2 1

INTRODUCTION

Life is full of anticipation as we look down life's road to see what the future has in store. Remember those eager days when you couldn't wait to get your driver's license? Or when you were a high school senior, and graduation day seemed to never arrive? Or those months, days, and hours you counted down toward your wedding day?

But for a long time in life, becoming a grandparent is not one of those "can't wait for it" moments. Family life is packed with enough excitement, drama, and ups and downs of its own for those two decades or so after the wedding. You are just trying to catch your breath and keep the family fed and clothed—not really anticipating getting to that age when you can hear someone call you "Grandma" or "Grandpa" without feeling insulted.

Yet almost suddenly it happens.

I still recall that phone call from my oldest daughter, Lisa, who had been married to her husband, Todd, for several years. In retrospect, it was funny how she introduced to me the concept of being a grandfather.

"Dad, we have a problem," she said.

I didn't expect that to be followed by "I'm pregnant."

At the time, she and Todd had been attempting to adopt, and they were confident that a baby boy was soon coming to join their family. So, Lisa's "problem" was that they would be going from no babies to two babies all at once.

As it turns out, the baby boy never arrived in their home, so we ended up celebrating just one grandchild that December day several years ago.

And despite not really cherishing the idea of being old enough to be a grandpa yet, when little Eliana Ruth was born, my heart melted.

And now, as she goes through her teen years, she still has a pretty good grip on my heart.

Becoming and being a grandparent, it turns out, is a marvelously special time of life. Several others have come along to join Eliana, and as Sue and I collect these special gifts from heaven, we are fabulously grateful for the joy they bring to our lives.

One popular grandparenting sign says, "Grandchildren fill a space in your heart that you never knew was empty." So true. You pour your life into your children, watch them grow up, and nurture them in godliness the best you can. You think they have your whole heart. And then children come into their homes, and you discover that your heart has new pockets of love. And the outpouring of that love showers those children every time you see them.

This book is a little bit about you and a little bit about them. And it's all about God—His love for you and for them. It captures both the joys of grandparenting and the jobs of grandparenting. And helps us celebrate being the most important older people in our grandchildren's lives.

Whether you are brand new or a veteran at spoiling and training and praying for your kids' kids, this book will encourage you and inspire you.

Written by a number of respected *Our Daily Bread* writers, these articles remind us of the godly responsibility we have to influence our grandkids for Jesus. They challenge us to think biblically about life as spiritual guides for our kids and their kids. They give us courage and hope for the times of difficulties we'll face. And they will always prompt us to stay true to our faith in Jesus Christ.

Each reading is designed to help you learn from God's Word and then spend some time with God in reflection, prayer, and planning for deep relationships during these marvelous years.

May God's blessings be with you as you cherish these bonus children God has allowed to join your family.

Dave Branon
General Editor
Moments with God for Grandparents

1

Building Bridges

Titus 2:1-6

Urge the younger women to love their husbands and children.

Titus 2:4

Grandparents are great bridge-builders. Perhaps our own grandparents, raised in a far different world from our own grandchildren today, relayed an important heritage of both history and faith down through the years. And now we can—though we grew up in an era not like the one our grandchildren are growing up in—convey the one truth that crosses all generations, regardless of the distractions: a testimony of faith in Jesus Christ.

In a sense, it seems strange that grandparents can have such far-reaching influence. After all, they are separated from their grandchildren by forty to seventy years or more. Yet grandparents often have an uncanny ability to bridge that generation gap—sometimes even better than parents can.

Older Christians, including grandparents, have a unique responsibility and opportunity—that of instruction, which either directly or indirectly keeps the heritage of faith going.

Let's be thankful for the strong heritage of faith, love, and family that grandparents can leave for those who come after them. And as grandparents, look for opportunities to relate to our grandchildren. Seek to bridge the generations so you can see the faith of our fathers become the faith of our children's children.

If you have had grandparents and parents who know the Lord, there is reason to be grateful for that heritage. And if you didn't, you can be grateful that a new string of faithfulness can start with you and your own family. Let your grandchildren see how important Jesus is to you—and the difference He can make in their lives.

Dear heavenly Father, I wonder what my family will look like in fifty years. I trust that there will be a heritage of faith in Jesus even into the next century—if Jesus does not return by then. Help me to do what I can to build that bridge.

Embrace the differences between the generations while pointing to what all people have in common: a need for Jesus.

2

A Lasting Purpose

John 21:15–25

Jesus said, "Feed my lambs."
John 21:15

Just two things from this life last throughout eternity. They are the Word of God (Matthew 24:35) and people (John 5:28–29). After all else is gone, they will still exist. So it makes sense that what we do in these few short years should be built around these two imperishables.

This is especially relevant for the believer in Jesus who is thinking about and planning for retirement or who has already settled into this welcome stage of life. This much-longed-for time is sometimes entered as if it's full-time fishing, golf, travel, and leisure—with little stimulation from new experiences.

However, a vague feeling of emptiness can take over if all we do is serve ourselves.

After Harold Sterling, a schoolteacher from Toronto, retired, a Christian physician told him, "Harold, you need a purpose. All your life you've worked with and loved people; you mustn't quit now!" And he didn't. Although Harold no longer worked with students in a classroom, as he did during his teaching career, he still loved people in his retirement. He found fulfillment in sharing the Word of God in hospital rooms as a chaplain.

When Jesus told Peter, "Feed my lambs" (John 21:15), He meant for Peter to keep doing it until the day he died. We don't need to feel guilty about enjoying a more leisurely pace and indulging in much-needed recreations, yet we can leave space to share God's Word with people who need it. It's the best of both worlds.

Thinking about retirement? Already there? What God-given skills did you use throughout your work life? You can use those same abilities to help others as you mix ministry with relaxation. God has a good plan for you, and you'll thank Him for it when you settle into the right routine.

Lord, direct my thinking as I figure out life in retirement. Help me to find the balance between slowing down and serving others.

> **To retire doesn't mean to quit.**
> **It's just a reassignment of time.**

3

For Future Generations

2 Timothy 1:1–7

I am reminded of your sincere faith, which
first lived in your grandmother Lois.

2 Timothy 1:5

When a team of Christians visited Stavropol, Russia, to hand out Bibles, a local citizen told them he recalled seeing Bibles in an old warehouse. They had been confiscated in the 1930s when Stalin was sending believers to the gulags. Amazingly, when they checked, the Bibles were still there.

Among those who showed up to load them into trucks was a young agnostic student just wanting to earn a day's wage. But soon he slipped away from the job to steal a Bible. A team member went looking for him and found him sitting in a corner weeping. Out of the hundreds of Bibles, he had picked up one that bore the handwritten signature of his own grandmother. Persecuted for her faith, she had no doubt prayed often for her family and her city. God used that grandmother's Bible to convict that young man.

God has no grandchildren. We must each become first-generation believers through personal faith in Jesus. But the devotion to God of a grandparent is a powerful ally of His Spirit to bring our children to Christ.

Paul encouraged Timothy by recalling the faith of his grandmother and mother. Although Timothy's faith was his own, it was deeply linked to theirs. What an encouragement to us who are grandparents to be faithful!

What a privilege you have as a grandparent to have spiritual input into a child's life. Because your salvation is the centerpiece of your life, you can influence your grandkids to recognize how important it should be in theirs. Sometimes giving them an age-appropriate Bible in which you have underlined key passages can help.

Lord, open windows of time when I can influence my grandchildren about how essential it is for them to have a relationship with you through Jesus. Give me the appropriate words at the right time.

A grandparent's faithfulness
could be just the encouragement
a grandchild needs to find out about Jesus.

4

Poor Example

Matthew 23:1-13

You must be careful to do everything they tell you. But do not do what they do, for they do not practice what they preach.

Matthew 23:3

A woman in Oregon was caught driving 103 miles per hour with her ten-year-old grandson in the car. When she was stopped by the police, she told them that she was only trying to teach him never to drive that fast. Perhaps she wanted him to do as she said, not as she did.

The Pharisees and teachers of the law seemed to have a similar problem. Jesus had a scathing assessment of them: They were spiritually bankrupt. He held these two groups directly responsible for this sad spiritual condition. As the successors of the lawgiver Moses, they were responsible for expounding the law so that people would walk in God's ways and have a genuine and vibrant relationship with the Lord (Deuteronomy 10:12–13). But their personal interpretation and application of the law became more important than God's law. They did not practice what they preached. Their obedience was done not to bring glory to God but to honor themselves. Jesus exposed who they were—image managers, posers, and hypocrites.

The effectiveness of following Jesus is not just in what we say but also in how we live. Let's model by words and actions what it means to follow Him.

Think back to the people who set a good example for you. A coach. A teacher. A parent. Maybe even a friend. And now it's your turn to set the example. You can show your gratitude for those who guided you by example by showing those younger than you and closest to you—your grandchildren—the way of truth. Role modeling for grandkids should be a top priority.

Dear Father, you know I'm not perfect. Despite my flaws, help me to model for my grandchildren the way of the godly. Honesty in dealing with people. Kindness when it is not easy. Love above all. Dedication to you as a lifestyle. Please help me to model for them what it means to follow you.

When we live "righteously" as a show, people won't see Jesus—just us.

5

Because of Love

James 2:14–26

You see that his faith and his actions were working together,
and his faith was made complete by what he did.

James 2:22

One day a dad came home from work to find a plate of peanut butter snack bars on the kitchen counter. Accompanying the delectables was a note from his twelve-year-old daughter to her grandparents. "Dear Grandma and Grandpa, I made these for you. Love, Melissa."

No one told her to do this. She didn't have to. She just did it.

But why? Was this preteen trying to gain their favor? Was she trying to make sure that they loved her? Was she trying to win Brownie points (well, snack-bar points) with her grandparents?

No, she cooked up this little confectionary delight just to show her grandparents she loves them. It was evidence of their close relationship. She did it because she *is* their granddaughter—not to somehow earn the right *to be* their granddaughter.

That's how it is with the good works we do as followers of Jesus Christ. We don't do good works so we can win a place in heaven. Rather, our good deeds show evidence of our salvation and faith in Christ.

Jesus did all the work of providing salvation. But we still have work to do. Why? Not to win His favor but to show our love. It's an outpouring of a grateful heart.

Look around at your world. What good works has God especially equipped you to do for others? Your gratitude for His provision of salvation shows when you serve others as He has equipped you to do.

Dear Lord, I realize I don't have to buy my salvation, but I can say thank you by using the opportunities you give me to advance your kingdom. Give me wisdom to know how to do that.

Because of God's gift of salvation,
we say thanks by sharing the gospel with others.

6

Following Our Example

1 Timothy 4:12–16

Don't let anyone look down on you because you are young, but set an example for the believers.

1 Timothy 4:12

Alyssa, who was six and just learning to read, often saw her parents and grandparents reading their Bibles in the morning. Early one day, she woke up before everyone else. When Grandma got up, she found Alyssa sitting on the couch with her Bible and a devotional booklet on her lap. She was following others' example of spending time with God at the beginning of the day.

Timothy, a young pastor, faced heavy responsibilities in the church at Ephesus—training believers, leading in worship, countering false doctrine. The older, more-experienced apostle Paul gave him instruction on leading the church in these areas, but he also mentioned the importance of personal conduct. He said, "Set an example for the believers in speech, in conduct, in love, in faith and in purity" (1 Timothy 4:12).

Paul challenged Timothy: "Watch your life and doctrine closely" (v. 16). If he paid attention to his own spiritual life and to solid doctrine, he would be a godly example to the church family.

We all have others who are observing us. We can see in Alyssa's story how older believers set the example for her—and the cycle goes on. Let's live in such a way that those who follow our example will help others in their walk with God.

Your words and actions can point your grandchildren to the Savior. What a privilege!

Dear heavenly Father, whether I have continual contact with my grandkids—or occasional opportunities— help me to be creative in setting the right example for them.

Being a living example of Jesus
can be our most effective witnessing tool.

7

"Compliments of the Author"

2 Peter 1:16–21

All Scripture is God-breathed and is useful for teaching, rebuking, correcting and training in righteousness.

2 Timothy 3:16

The story is told about an elementary-school-age boy who was planning to give his grandmother a Bible for her birthday. He wanted to write something special to her in the front of the Bible but wasn't sure what to say. So, he decided to copy what he had seen in a book his father had received from a friend.

Grandma's birthday arrived, and she opened her gift. She was not only pleased to receive the Bible but also amused by the inscription her grandson had put in it. It read: "To Grandma, with compliments of the author."

Even though that young boy was unaware of it, he had suggested a unique fact about the Bible. It does come compliments of the author—and that author is God. The apostle Paul wrote, "All Scripture is God-breathed" (2 Timothy 3:16). And Peter said, "Prophets, though human, spoke from God as they were carried along by the Holy Spirit" (2 Peter 1:21). That makes the Bible the most valuable and desirable of all books.

Knowing who wrote a book often determines whether we'll pick it up and read it. The Bible, with its divine origin, not only ought to be read but also demands our respect, our trust, and our obedience. It comes "with compliments of the Author."

Take a few minutes to study the authorship of Scripture to help solidify in your mind that it is truly God's Word. Some verses to start with are 2 Timothy 3:16; 2 Peter 1:21; 1 Corinthians 2:12–13; and Hebrews 4:12. The more you understand God's authorship, the greater will be your appreciation for this remarkable book.

Dear Lord, thank you for preserving this book—the most amazing one ever authored. Thank you that it tells the gospel message and gives us guidelines for how to live for you.

> The Bible is unique above all books, for it alone is inspired by the One who knows just what we need.

8

When Everything Goes Wrong

Genesis 42:1-7, 25-36

Jacob said to them, ". . . Everything is against me!"
Genesis 42:36

Poor Jacob had reached the end of his rope. Hearing upsetting news from his sons who had just returned from Egypt, he said in utter dismay, "Everything is against me!" (Genesis 42:36).

His son Joseph had been taken from him. Famine was plaguing the land of Canaan. Simeon was being held as a hostage. And now Benjamin, the youngest son, was being demanded as a ransom to secure his brother's release. That was almost too much for the aging patriarch to bear. Overwhelmed by these circumstances, he felt that everything had turned against him. In reality, however, God was working out His wise purposes.

When the dust of Jacob's turmoil finally began to settle, it became increasingly clear that all these distressing events were indeed intended for his ultimate good. They led to his move to Egypt where the Lord made his family into a great nation. Even though Jacob had declared that everything was against him, from God's standpoint everything was going for him.

When everything seems to be going wrong, dwell on the truth that "in all things God works for the good of those who love him" (Romans 8:28).

Then, instead of sounding like Jacob, you'll be able to say confidently, "God is working for me!"

Pause and reflect on some times when things seemed to be going sideways for you but in the end God worked things out for good. Surely He can do that again, as promised in Romans 8. God's care for you is something you can share with your grandkids. Your thankfulness for God's hand in your life could challenge them to think differently about the problems they face.

Dear Lord, thank you for your care for my life—
even when I might have thought things were out
of hand. Help me to use your dealings in my life
as a testimony to others of your goodness.

> It's impossible for "everything to go wrong"
> when God is in control.

9

Well Loved

1 John 4:7–21

We love Him because He first loved us.

1 John 4:19 NKJV

A man described his grandmother as one of the greatest influences in his life. Throughout his adult years, he kept her portrait next to his desk to remind himself of her unconditional love. "I really do believe," he told a friend, "that my grandmother helped me learn how to love."

Not everyone has had a similar taste of human love, but through Christ each of us can experience being well loved by God. In 1 John 4, the word *love* occurs twenty-seven times, and God's love through Christ is cited as the source of our love for God and for others. "This is love: not that we loved God, but that he loved us and sent his Son as an atoning sacrifice for our sins" (v. 10). "We know and rely on the love God has for us" (v. 16). "We love Him because He first loved us" (v. 19 NKJV).

God's love is not a slowly dripping faucet or a well we must dig for ourselves. It is a rushing stream that flows from His heart into ours. Whatever our family background or experiences in life—whether we feel well loved by others or not—we can know love. We can draw from the Lord's inexhaustible source to know His loving care for us, and we can pass it on to others.

In Christ our Savior, we are well loved.

What a great feeling it is to be well loved. Do you feel that way? Even if humans don't quite come through in the love department, you can know that our Savior does. God loved us first—and always will.

Dear Lord, I am not always lovable, yet you overlook my unloveliness! You saw me as redeemed a long time ago, and you see me as your child. What amazing love you have for me. Help me to mirror that love to the special people in my life—especially my grandchildren.

The love of God that flows to us from Him can stream out of our lives into the lives of those we influence.

10

Why Worship?

Psalm 27

Wait for the LORD; be strong and take
heart and wait for the LORD.

Psalm 27:14

Why bother going to church? Some would tell us that it's better to sleep late on Sunday, eat a leisurely breakfast, and lounge around talking with the family. And then maybe have lunch with friends or enjoy a picnic and games with the children. "Make it a day that's different and even restful," some would say, "but don't waste time by going to church on Sunday!"

Worship? Who needs worship anyway?

We all do! We need worship because we are unique creatures made in the image of God. We are made for God, so we can't fulfill our purpose unless we develop a right relationship with Him. And the teaching, fellowship, and worship we enjoy with other believers help us to do that when we focus on the Lord.

As we join with other worshipers in church, our hearts are lifted out of this temporal world into God's eternal world. According to William Temple, in worship the *conscience* is quickened by the holiness of God, the *mind* is fed by the truth of God, the *imagination* is purged by the beauty of God, the *heart* is opened to the love of God, and the *will* is devoted to the purpose of God. This helps us in our goal of becoming more Christlike in our daily living.

Let's decide now that this Sunday—and as often as we are able—we will be in church with a heart prepared to worship, fellowship, and learn.

Because the believer's church experience is truly about focusing on Jesus and what He has done for you, it's easily the best place to go to praise Him and lift up your heart in gratitude to Him. Think of the church as a special place where you join with others to learn about God and find new ways to say "Thank you" to Him.

Dear Lord, thank you for both the universal church throughout time and the local church, where we gather in your name. Help me to get the most out of every visit as I worship with my friends and family.

No activity we undertake has as much value as worship— for it feeds everything else we do.

11

Honest to God

Isaiah 1:12–18

Then I acknowledged my sin to you and
did not cover up my iniquity.

Psalm 32:5

A woman's three-year-old grandson's day was off to a rotten start. He couldn't find his favorite shirt. The shoes he wanted to wear were too hot. He fussed and fumed at his grandmother and then sat down to cry.

"Why are you so upset?" she asked. They talked for a while and after he calmed down, she gently inquired, "Have you been good for Grandma?" He looked thoughtfully at his shoes and responded, "No, I was bad. I'm sorry."

The grandma's heart went out to him. Instead of denying what he had done, he was honest. In the following moments they quietly asked Jesus to forgive them when they did wrong and asked Him to help them do better.

In Isaiah 1, God confronts His people about wrongs they had committed. Bribes and injustice were rampant in the courts, and orphans and widows were taken advantage of for material gain. Yet even then God responded mercifully, asking the people of Judah to confess what they had done and turn from it: "Come now, let us settle the matter. . . . Though your sins are like scarlet, they shall be as white as snow" (Isaiah 1:18).

God longs for us to be open with Him about our sins. He meets honesty and repentance with loving forgiveness: "If we confess our sins, he is faithful and just and will forgive us our sins and purify us from all unrighteousness" (1 John 1:9). Because our God is merciful, new beginnings await!

Even grandparents do wrong from time to time—but they can be thankful that God is still faithful after all these years. They can be grateful that God wants them to "settle the matter" so He can keep forgiving them.

Lord, search my heart. Help me to keep my slate clean through forgiveness, as an example to the younger ones who are looking up to me. Help me to be open with you about my failings.

> Living with guilt is far worse than living with confession. Confession leads to the mercy of the One who erases our guilt.

12

God's Provisions

2 Kings 4:1-7

Elisha replied to her, "How can I help you? Tell
me, what do you have in your house?"

2 Kings 4:2

Three-year-old Buddy and his mom went to church each week to help unload groceries from the food ministry truck. When Buddy overheard his mom telling his grandmother that the delivery truck broke down, he said, "Oh no. How will they do food ministry?" His mom explained that the church would have to raise money to buy a new truck.

Buddy smiled. "I have money," he said, leaving the room. He returned with a plastic jar decorated with colorful stickers and filled with coins, which amounted to a little over $38. Though Buddy didn't have much, God combined his sacrificial offering with gifts from others to provide a new refrigerated truck, so that the church could continue serving their community.

A small amount offered generously is always more than enough when placed in God's hands. In 2 Kings 4, a poor widow asked the prophet Elisha for financial assistance. He told her to take inventory of her own resources, reach out to her neighbors for help, then follow his instructions (vv. 1–4). In a miraculous display of provision, God used the widow's small amount of oil to fill all the jars she collected from her neighbors

(vv. 5–6). Elisha told her, "Sell the oil and pay your debts. You and your sons can live on what is left" (v. 7).

When we focus on what we don't have, we risk missing out on watching God do great things with what He has given us.

Sometimes grandchildren can teach lessons about simple obedience. Look for those little ways your grandkids show that they understand generosity. Then compliment them and pray with them, thanking God for their young wisdom.

Dear God, at this stage of life, I need to stop and thank you for providing for me for so many years. Help me to be even more generous with my time, my talents, and even my money. Help me to avoid missing out on what you are trying to teach me in these areas.

We give what we can, and we let God handle the rest.

13

Elm or Evergreen?

2 Samuel 6:1–5

Ephraim, what more have I to do with idols? I will
answer him and care for him. I am like a flourishing
juniper; your fruitfulness comes from me.

Hosea 14:8

Early one fall, so the story goes, while the leaves were still on
the trees, there was an exceptionally heavy snowstorm. Rachel's
grandfather took her for a drive and said, "Notice those elm trees.
The branches are so badly broken that the trees may die. But just look
at those pines and evergreens. The storm didn't hurt them at all. Rachel,
there are two kinds of trees in the world: the foolish and the wise. An
elm holds its branches rigid. As it becomes weighted down, eventually
its limbs break. But when an evergreen is loaded, it simply relaxes, low-
ers its branches, and lets the burden slip away. It remains unharmed. Try
to be like a pine tree."

Christians who give up all their cares to the Lord can face life's burdens much better than those who try to bear the weight themselves. The
apostle Paul, who experienced many trials and adversities, gave a three-
fold method for handling difficulties: (1) Be anxious for nothing. (2) Pray
about everything. (3) Give thanks for anything (Philippians 4:6).

You can be like the elm tree that tries to bear all its troubles, only to
break under the load. Or you can be like a pine tree because you roll all
your burdens on the Lord. Be like a pine tree!

What is something—some care or some feeling for someone else—that you have been holding on to like a stubborn elm tree? Re-read Paul's words in Philippians 4:5–7 and see that it is possible to let go. Then rejoice in the joy you feel by letting go of what had been weighing you down.

Dear Lord, you know my heart. You know that I am still hanging on to _____ and _____. Help me to let them slide off my heart and into your capable hands.

True faith causes us to cast our burdens on Jesus, just as He told us to, believing that He meant what He said.

14

"I Remember, Grandpa"

Mark 10:13-16

And he took the children in his arms, placed
his hands on them and blessed them.

Mark 10:16

Five-year-old Bree climbed up onto her grandpa's lap. She snuggled close to him and whispered, "I remember what you told me, Grandpa." Her words brought warm assurance to his heart.

Here's why. As a grandfather, he had decided to be a good influence for Christ to his grandchildren. He didn't preach at them or badger them, but he simply talked to them about the Lord. He and Bree had been talking one day, and she told him she was memorizing some verses. So he helped her to see how the verses she was learning could apply to her, even as a little girl.

He asked her to recite John 3:16, one of the verses she had memorized. He told her to substitute her name for the words "the world" and "whoever." Then he told her why—because God loved her, and Christ died for her. After listening intently and doing what he suggested, she went on her way. Now it was a few months later, and that's why this grandpa was so happy that she remembered. She knew that Jesus loved her.

You don't have to be a theologian to tell a child about the Lord. Just be willing to sit next to your grandchild and give him or her the best blessing of all—the message of God's love.

The grandpa in today's story was grateful that little Bree had recalled what he taught her. You can have that same feeling as you nudge your grandchildren toward Jesus and truth in small ways. They cannot have too many positive influences: Christian teachers, parents, godly friends—and Grandma and Grandpa. What a privilege!

Dear heavenly Father, give me wisdom to convey
to my children's children some important lessons
that will move them toward godliness. Help me to
know how to do this in the most effective way.

Grand adventures await when grandchildren hear the greatest story ever told from their grandparents.

15

Snapshots of Heaven

1 Thessalonians 4:13–18

We who are still alive and are left will be caught up together
with them in the clouds to meet the Lord in the air.

1 Thessalonians 4:17

A father asked his ten-year-old son, "Why do you want to go to heaven?" He expected to hear something about streets of gold or not having to go to school or something similar. Instead, he said, "Because I want to see Grandpa."

It had been several years since the youngster's grandpa had gone to be with the Lord. But time didn't seem to diminish how much he admired and missed his Army veteran grandfather. That's why the fact that he knew he would see him again in heaven was so important to him.

The prospect of heaven is one of the most comforting truths in the Bible. Not only can we find hope in knowing that we will someday be in Jesus's presence, but we can also anticipate seeing loved ones who are waiting for us on the other side (1 Thessalonians 4:14, 17).

Imagine a grieving widow who has the assurance of being reunited with her husband of fifty years. Imagine sorrowing parents knowing that their child who succumbed to disease will be reunited with them. What a wonderful hope!

The promise of reunion in heaven gives us a glimpse of what our eternal home will be like. The prospect of seeing the people we love gives us snapshots of heaven in an album of hope.

Think for a moment about who you want to see in heaven—someone close to you who has already joined Jesus in glory. The fact that you have the sure hope of a reunion someday is a reason for intense gratitude to your great God. Imagine seeing both Jesus and your departed loved one. Truly awesome!

Dear Lord, thank you for hope. Hope in this life through the guidance and help of the Holy Spirit, and hope for the next life as we have the confidence of grand reunions. May I live in those messages of hope with renewed joy.

We may not know the details of our heavenly reunion, but that doesn't dampen our enthusiasm for that future reality.

16

Questions

Joshua 4:1–18

But in your hearts revere Christ as Lord. Always be
prepared to give an answer to everyone who asks you
to give the reason for the hope that you have.

1 Peter 3:15

A young boy was in a church service with his grandfather. Full
of curiosity, the boy kept asking, "What does *that* mean?"
Grandpa quietly explained everything that was going on.
When the pastor began his sermon, he took off his watch and placed it
on the podium. The boy whispered, "What does that mean?" Grandpa,
who had heard many long sermons that sent the service into overtime,
answered, "Not a thing, Mikey. Not a thing."

That's a funny story, but there's a serious side to it. The boy's barrage
of questions may have irritated some people, but the grandfather knew
that children have an inquisitive nature that makes them open to spiritual truth.

Israel's leader Joshua knew that too. He knew that children of future
generations would ask about the pile of stones that he was told to place
in the Jordan River as the people of Israel crossed into the Promised
Land. So he told parents to use the opportunity to tell how God had
miraculously parted the waters of the Jordan (Joshua 4:6–7).

Questions—even simple ones from the children in our family—can
open the door to explaining important matters of faith. If we are clear

and inviting when those questions arise, our grandchildren will notice. Our willingness to try to guide them will open the door to valuable conversations. Let the questions begin.

Sometimes children and teens are willing to ask questions of Grandpa and Grandma that they might not ask of someone else. So keep that door wide open, and be grateful for the unique relationship you share with those precious kids.

Lord, help me to be the kind of grandparent who listens
and doesn't always talk—indicating to my grandchildren
that I am safe to talk with. Give me answers or
wisdom to find them when the opportunities arise.

The curiosity of a child combined with the wisdom of a grandparent is a powerful teaching tool.

17

Legacy
of Forgiveness

1 John 2:1-12

Your sins have been forgiven on account of his name.

1 John 2:12

Five years after World War II ended, Marvin Maris met Taizo Fujishiro at a theological seminary in Chicago. Even though the men had served on opposite sides during the bitter conflict, Maris befriended Fujishiro, typed class notes for him, taught him to drive, and invited him to his home for Christmas. After Fujishiro returned to Japan, they stayed in touch.

Four decades later, Maris's granddaughter, Connie Wieck, went to Japan to teach English. She phoned Fujishiro and introduced herself. The next day they met for lunch, and the man told her all about her grandfather—his first American friend.

Connie later wrote: "Growing up in a town whose veterans were still bitter . . . , I had come to believe that forgiveness was beyond any first-hand witnesses to that history. The lasting friendship between my grandfather and Taizo proved otherwise."

The apostle Paul described the marvel of salvation by writing, "While we were God's enemies, we were reconciled to him through the death of his Son" (Romans 5:10). And John said that those who are forgiven are to love others (1 John 2:9–12). No restrictions on who we should forgive—even war enemies.

As we humbly receive God's gift of mercy in Christ, the all-important legacy of forgiveness can extend into places we could never otherwise imagine. In a world of growing individual animosity, we need forgiveness now more than ever. Let's pass it on to all.

In a lifetime of interacting with others, it's easy to accumulate an "I can't forgive that person" list. Out of a deep appreciation for God's forgiveness, you can work on whittling that list down to zero. The Holy Spirit has the power to help you do that.

Lord, open my eyes to see where I may have neglected to forgive someone: family, friends, coworkers. Guide me to do what you did for me in Jesus—forgive completely. Help me to enjoy that freedom.

Offering forgiveness to others opens up avenues for surprising new friendships.

18

Just Watch

1 Corinthians 4:14-17

Follow my example, as I follow the example of Christ.

1 Corinthians 11:1

The young boy looked up at his grandfather and wondered aloud, "Grandpa, how do you live for Jesus?" The grandfather, highly respected in his community and church, stooped down and quietly told the boy, "Just watch."

As the years went by, the grandfather was an example to the boy of how to follow Jesus. He stayed rock-steady in living for Him. Yet the grandson often lived in a way that was not pleasing to God.

One day the young man visited his grandfather for what both knew would be the last time. As the older man lay dying, his grandson leaned over the bed and heard his grandpa whisper, "Did you watch?"

That was the turning point in the boy's life. He understood that when his grandpa had said, "Just watch," he meant, "Follow my example, as I follow the example of Christ" (1 Corinthians 11:1). He vowed that from then on, he would live as his grandfather did—striving to please Jesus. He had watched, and now he knew how to live.

Somebody is watching you. Probably more somebodies than you even know. Younger Christians need to see that it is possible to live for Jesus every day and in every way, and you can show them the way. Challenge them—and yourself. Challenge them to "just watch."

What a great privilege it is to lead the way for others. Take the "just watch" challenge for yourself, vowing to lead the way in faithful living for your grandchildren to see. In words and action, show them Jesus. Then look forward to the day when they say "thank you."

Dear Lord, despite my own schedule and my own interests, help me to carve out time for example-setting with my grandchildren. Guide me to show them in words, in service, and in dedication what a Christ-follower looks like.

A grandparent's example may be all a grandchild needs to edge them toward faith and godly living.

19

Music Inside

Psalm 98

Shout for joy to the LORD, all the earth,
burst into jubilant song with music.

Psalm 98:4

Singing came naturally to the four von Trapp children. They are the great-grandchildren of Captain Georg von Trapp, whose romance with his second wife, Maria, inspired the 1965 movie *The Sound of Music*.

After their grandfather Werner von Trapp had a stroke, the Montana-based siblings recorded their first CD in order to cheer him up. Soon the children were performing around the world. They retired from full-time singing in 2016. Stefan, the children's father, said of them, "The music is inside them."

The writer of Psalm 98 also had a song in his heart. He called on others to join him in singing "to the LORD a new song, for he has done marvelous things" (v. 1). The psalmist praised God for His salvation, His righteousness, His mercy, and His faithfulness (vv. 2–3). The psalmist's heart was so overflowing with praise that he called on the earth to break forth in song, the rivers to clap their hands, and the hills to be joyful (vv. 4, 8).

We have much to be thankful for as well—God's good gifts of family and friends, and His daily supply for our needs. He faithfully cares for us, His children.

Unlike the von Trapp singers, we may not be able to sing well. But when we recall all that God is to us and all that He has done for us, we can't help but "burst into jubilant song" (v. 4) anyway. The music is inside. Let it out.

Music is a good thing to share with grandchildren. Sometimes you may introduce them to the "oldies" of your era, but you should also share with them the Christ-centered music that has influenced you. That music helped you, and perhaps it will help them as well.

Dear Lord, thank you for music. Help me to never tire of singing your praises, and help me to show my grandchildren the value of godly music and praise. May the music that is inside my heart because of you spread from me to others.

> **When a song in our hearts makes it to our lips, others can see the joy of Jesus.**

20

What Do We Want?

Romans 8:1–11

He who raised Christ from the dead will also give life to
your mortal bodies because of his Spirit who lives in you.

Romans 8:11

I went from the horse-and-buggy to moon walks and computers," said
the elderly man to his granddaughter as he tried to put his life into
perspective. But then he mused, "I never thought it would be so short."

Life *is* short, so we turn to Jesus because we want to live forever. That's
not bad, but perhaps we don't comprehend what eternal life really is. We
long for something better, and we think it's just ahead. *If only I had more
money. If only I lived by a lake. If only I could take a European vacation. If
only* . . . And then one day we catch an echo of that grandfather's voice.

The truth is, we possess eternal life *now*. The apostle Paul wrote, "The
law of the Spirit who gives life has set you free from the law of sin and
death" (Romans 8:2). Then he said, "Those who live in accordance with
the Spirit have their minds set on what the Spirit desires" (v. 5). In other
words, our desires change when we come to Christ. This naturally gives
us what we most desire. "The mind governed by the Spirit is life and
peace" (v. 6).

It's one of life's great lies that we need to be somewhere else, doing
something else, with someone else before we start truly living. When we
find our life in Jesus, we exchange regret over life's brevity for the full
enjoyment of life with Him, both now and forever.

When you were young, life looked like an endless adventure. Now, looking back, you can easily wonder *Where did it all go?* And *What do I still have ahead?* You can be grateful that God is with you in the now, and your daily living right now has tremendous value. Enjoying life starts today—from now until eternity with God.

> *Heavenly Father, thank you for this life. Help me to make the most of each day—not pining for what might have been or bemoaning something I don't have. Jesus said that He brought "life to the full." Help me to live fully.*

Although we can't experience heaven on earth in this life, having heaven in our heart adds joy to our day-to-day existence.

21

When Love Never Ends

Psalm 145:8–20

The LORD watches over all who love him.
Psalm 145:20

W henever my grandfather took me to the beach," Sandra reminisced, "he always took off his watch and put it away. One day I asked him why. He smiled and replied, 'Because I want you to know how important my moments with you are to me. I just want to be with you and let time go by.'"

Sandra shared that recollection at her grandfather's funeral. She said it was one of her favorite memories of their life together. As we reflect on how valued it makes us feel when others take time for us, we can find even greater hope in some Bible passages about God's loving care.

God always makes time for us. David prayed in Psalm 145:16–18, "You open your hand and satisfy the desires of every living thing. The LORD is righteous in all his ways and faithful in all he does. The LORD is near to all who call on him."

God's goodness and thoughtful attention sustain our lives each moment. He provides us with air to breathe and food to eat. Because He is rich in love, the Creator of all things mercifully crafts even the most intricate details of our existence.

God's love is deep and unending. It is such a spacious love that in His kindness and mercy He's opened the way to both eternal life and joy in His presence, as if to say, "I love you so much, I just want to be with you forever, and let time go by."

There is so much to be thankful for! God's generosity, His sustaining goodness, His fathomless love. Sandra's grandpa took off his watch to demonstrate human generosity. What can you do to show your grandkids such godly characteristics?

Righteous God, sometimes I go through life without giving you much thought. Help me to pause and express my sincere gratitude to you for watching over me, lavishing your love on me, and helping me to spread your goodness to following generations of people who need you so much.

The world offers no equal to a life enhanced by God's presence, His goodness, and His love.

22

The Age of Adventure

Deuteronomy 34:1–7

Moses was a hundred and twenty years old when he died, yet his eyes were not weak nor his strength gone.

Deuteronomy 34:7

Adventure is often associated with youth. But older people too can retain a sense of wonder and expectation about life. Moses, for example, was 120 years old when he climbed Mount Nebo. As he reached the top, a vast and beautiful land spread out before him. That breathtaking panorama must have stirred him deeply as he saw all that God had promised to Israel. The ascent to Nebo's summit that day must have been almost as thrilling as the high moments of Mount Sinai. Moses kept looking forward—his faith clearly focused on God's promises.

Author Gladys Hunt wrote: "People who stand still in life, closed up tight against whatever God might offer, never learn how to let anything important happen to them. Time just runs itself out. It takes courage to put first things first, to risk new adventure, to rearrange existence. . . . The adventure of life is not finished. In God's plan for us there is always something new, something exciting and wonderful. The past is an apprenticeship for a new adventure, a new rhythm."

No matter where we are in life, we don't have to settle for an "on the shelf" existence. We're not like some sports trophy we won in high school that just sits there gathering dust and reminding us of past glories. No, we need to climb new mountains; claim fresh promises; do great things for God.

By seeking His will and trusting Him, we'll find that any age can be the age of adventure.

How thankful we can be that God gives us life. And you can be thankful that because He has you here, He has things for you to do. So, whether you are serving God specifically or simply enjoying life in the everyday—adventure awaits. Praise God for new days and ways to face challenges.

Dear Lord, no matter my physical condition, you have not left me here to sit and watch the world go by. Help me to find new adventures for your glory and new challenges to keep life fascinating. Help me, like Moses, to keep climbing.

Looking at each new day as an adventure of God's grace is a sure cure for dull and listless living.

Higher Goals

Numbers 8:23–26

They may assist their brothers in performing their duties.

Numbers 8:26

The first people to climb Mount Everest, the world's highest mountain, were Edmund Hillary and his Sherpa guide Tenzing Norgay in 1953. Hillary, from New Zealand, was just thirty-three years old. His feat afforded him fame, wealth, and the realization that he had already lived a remarkable life.

So, what did Hillary do for the next fifty-five years? Did he retire and rest on his laurels? Absolutely not.

Although Hillary had no higher mountains to climb, that didn't stop him. He achieved other notable goals, including an effort to improve the welfare of the Nepalese people living near Everest—a task he carried on until his death in 2008.

We sometimes hear that retirement isn't mentioned in the Bible. But it is! God told the Levites to retire from their regular duties at age fifty (Numbers 8:24–25). But He did not want them to stop helping others. He said that they should "assist their brothers" (v. 26). We cannot take this incident as a complete teaching on retirement (if you are fifty, you might wish so), but we can see a godly implication here. Continuing to serve others after our official "working days" are over is a good idea.

Even in retirement or near-retirement, we can continue to have higher goals. As the Levites and Sir Edmund Hillary did, we can refocus when we retire—giving of our time to help others.

Reaching the age of retirement is a reason to express gratitude to God. It's a time to realize that God gave you a lifetime of important work to do for your fellow man. And it's a time to seek God's guidance to reach higher goals—goals that keep your influence on those around you growing.

Dear Lord, give me examples of men or women in my circle of influence who can teach me how to retire successfully, people who dedicate their new free time to others—for your glory.

We need a spiritual counselor as much as a financial counselor if we want to retire in a godly way.

24

Pass It On

Deuteronomy 4:5–10

Watch yourselves closely so that you do not forget
the things your eyes have seen. . . . Teach them to
your children and to their children after them.

Deuteronomy 4:9

A grandmother was babysitting her preschool granddaughter
when she decided to share an old, familiar friend with her.
With the child in her arms, the grandmother picked up a well-
worn book that she had read to her daughter—the child's mother—
when she was a little girl. It was a book called *The Bible in Pictures for
Little Eyes*, a staple in that family's efforts to share God's truth with their
children—and now their baby granddaughter.

It was that child's turn to begin to learn about God's creation, His
goodness, His plan, and His salvation. It was time for her to be told
about what her mom's family had seen and experienced in their faith
walk. As Deuteronomy 4:9 says, "Teach [God's statutes] to your children and to their children after them."

Back in the days of Deuteronomy, the people were being handed a
gift from God—"the decrees and laws" (v. 1) that would allow them to
live properly in the land of God's promise. Along with those laws came
an admonition for the people to share with their progeny the lessons
God taught them on the way. They were told not to "forget the things

your eyes have seen" (v. 9), but to teach God's words and works to their children and grandchildren.

We have a similar legacy today. This is one of our greatest responsibilities as followers of Christ. Pass it on.

Do you have spiritual artifacts from your children's childhood? Can you use them in a new era to guide the next generation? Your grandchildren might be thrilled to know that their mommy or daddy heard from those same sources when they were little. Let the circle of God's love surround your grandchildren as it did your children.

Dear heavenly Father, thank you for the example of the Old Testament Israelites, who used family ties and historical object lessons to keep your story alive. Now it is my turn to pass along the faith in new and modern ways. Help me to find effective ways to do so.

There are few greater joys than sharing faith and godliness with impressionable, eager grandchildren.

A Good Man

Romans 15:1–13

A good name is more desirable than great riches.

Proverbs 22:1

While staying in a hotel in a small town, a preacher noticed that the church across the street was having a service. People were jammed into the church with a standing-room-only crowd of both young and old flowing out onto the sidewalk. When the visitor to the town noticed a hearse by the curb, he realized that the service was a funeral. And given the crowd, he assumed that it was the celebration of the life of some local hero—perhaps a wealthy businessperson or a famous personality. Curious, he said to the desk clerk, "That's an amazing turnout for a funeral; it must be for a famous person in town."

"No," he replied. "He wasn't rich or famous, but he was a good man."

This reminded the pastor of the wisdom of the proverb that says, "A good name is more desirable than great riches" (Proverbs 22:1). Indeed, it's a good idea to think about what kind of legacy we are leaving for our family, friends, and neighbors. From God's perspective it's not our resumé or the amount of money we've accumulated that matters but rather the kind of life we have lived.

One daughter, writing about her father who had just passed away, penned: "This world has lost a righteous man and in this world that is no small thing!" That's the kind of legacy we should be seeking for the glory of God.

Imagine how grateful that girl was that she had a dad about whom she could make such a wonderful comment. The world needs more people like him. Then imagine for a moment what someone might write about you. You can be thankful that it's never too late to make changes in your life and legacy.

Dear Lord, help people to remember me as a good person.
Not for me. But for you. Help them to see in me someone
who shines the light of Jesus on the world around me.

Greatness comes in all sizes, but none bigger
than a legacy of truth, love, and godliness.

26

What Is a Friend?

John 15:15–27

I no longer call you servants. . . . Instead,
I have called you friends.

John 15:15

Socrates once asked a simple old man what he was most thankful for. The man replied, "That being such as I am, I have had the friends I have had."

Some "friends" are fickle. In the book of Proverbs we read, "Wealth attracts many friends, but even the closest friend of the poor person deserts them" (19:4). A true friend, however, "loves at all times" (17:17) and "sticks closer than a brother" (18:24).

Our English word *friend* comes from the same root as the word *freedom*. A genuine friend sets us free to be who and what we are. We can pour out our doubts and talk freely about the wolves howling at the door of our life.

A faithful friend also affirms our worth. England's Queen Victoria (1819–1901) said of prime minister William Gladstone, "When I am with him, I feel I am *with* one of the most important leaders in the world." But of Benjamin Disraeli, another prime minister of the United Kingdom, she said, "He makes me feel as if I *am* one of the most important leaders of the world."

Christians have an inside track on making and being friends because we are part of one family. Haven't you felt that family tie while talking with a stranger—only to discover that you had Christ in common? And no wonder—He is the truest Friend anyone can have.

How important is it to have good friends at your stage of life? The best way to have friends is to be one. Take a moment to evaluate your friend situation. Thank God for those you have and enjoy—and perhaps ask Him to open up new friendships for you.

Dear Jesus, thank you that you are the greatest friend I could have. Guide me to be a constant, helpful friend. Help me to model for my grandchildren how to be a good friend.

No one lacks friends who is friends with Jesus.

27

Designed for Companionship

Ecclesiastes 4:7–12

A cord of three strands is not quickly broken.
Ecclesiastes 4:12

We don't function well as loners. Perhaps we've seen an old high school friend who became an unhappy recluse. Then there's that person who becomes angry with something small that happened at church, stopped attending services, and rejected old friends. He says he needs no one except God. Yet he becomes a miserable old man who suffers alone when bad things happen.

In Ecclesiastes 4:8 we read about a lonely person who devoted all his energy to the pursuit of wealth. He didn't have time for friends or family. He worked very hard, yet his wealth didn't satisfy the void in his life.

After depicting the lonely man, the author of Ecclesiastes illustrated the advantages of fellowship and partnership (vv. 9–12). He did so by referring to the value and productivity of two people working together (v. 9), of one helping the other when one falls (v. 10), of two keeping each other warm on cold nights (v. 11), and of two protecting each other when attacked (v. 12). The closing example, "A cord of three strands is not quickly broken," was a proverbial way of saying "there is strength in numbers."

God has designed us with a need for one another. We need to value family and keep them close. And it's wise to avoid letting little annoyances alienate us from those we love most. Think of the joys that come from fulfilling God's design for companionship.

Friends can irritate you. Family members can sometimes get on your last nerve. These annoyances can help you refocus your attention on a new approach. You can pray for friends and family. You can do something good for them. You can in all ways seek the Holy Spirit's help—and then thank the Lord for keeping unbroken the "cord of three strands."

> *Dear gracious Father, I need some of that grace you*
> *demonstrate and offer us. You know how irritated I*
> *get with people I need to keep close. Give me wisdom*
> *to stay connected and to demonstrate godly love.*

No squabble or disagreement is as important as the friendship it jeopardizes.

28

Older or Better?

2 Corinthians 4:16-18

We do not lose heart. Though outwardly we are wasting away, yet inwardly we are being renewed day by day.

2 Corinthians 4:16

We know we're getting older when we say things like, "Can you believe how young those schoolteachers are?" And it's a sure sign of aging when we no longer hear people ask, "How are you?" but instead say to us, "Hey, you look terrific"—as if they're surprised.

Aging is inevitable. Unfortunately, society has taught us to fear advancing age and to disguise its reality as much as possible. But aging can actually be a wonderful thing. Followers of Jesus have the capacity to get significantly better with age. As Paul put it: "Though outwardly we are wasting away, yet inwardly we are being renewed day by day" (2 Corinthians 4:16).

Just as there are physical signs that reveal we're getting older, there are signs that show we are getting better. Rather than becoming more crotchety, intolerant, and unloving, the maturing follower of Jesus grows better at forgiving, loving, and caring. Growing older is a continuation of the journey to become more like Jesus, which means that as time goes on, our heart and attitudes should increasingly resonate with and reflect the compelling character and winsome ways of our Savior.

So, as we grow older, let's embrace the opportunity to become spiritually more like Jesus. Our friends will notice that we look better with age.

You could bemoan getting older, or you could thank the Lord for giving you long life. It's all in the perspective. And since you are still on this incredible journey, you may as well be a positive force. You can encourage others. Offer smiles. Lend a hand when possible. Love Jesus more. The list could go on. Maybe it should—in a journal where you keep track of how you are getting better with age, by God's grace.

Dear Lord, I'm not crazy about the aging process.
But I am grateful for the many days you've given me
on this planet. Help me to come to grips with reality
while seeking new ways to reflect Jesus to others.

> The best way to "look" better is to look more and more like Jesus.

29

The Gift of Sleep

Psalm 127

In vain you rise early and stay up late, toiling for food
to eat—for he grants sleep to those he loves.

Psalm 127:2

Sleep is essential for good health. Scientists don't know exactly why we need it, but they know what happens when we don't get enough. We put ourselves at risk of premature aging, weight gain, and diseases ranging from colds and flu to cancer. What God accomplishes in our bodies while we are in dreamland is nothing short of miraculous. While we do nothing, God replenishes our energy, rebuilds and restores our cells, and reorganizes information in our brains.

The reasons for not getting enough sleep are many, and some we can't solve; but the Bible indicates that overwork should not be one of them (Psalm 127:2). Sleep is a gift from God that we should receive with gratitude. If we're not getting enough, we need to find out why. Are we rising early and staying up late to earn money to acquire things we don't need? Are we involved in ministry efforts that we think no one else is capable of doing?

I'm sometimes tempted to believe that the work I do when I'm awake is more important than the work God does while I sleep. But refusing God's gift of sleep is like telling Him that my work is more important than His.

God does not want anyone to be a slave to work. He wants us to enjoy His gift of sleep.

What a refreshing idea! In a world where "work harder" is often the mantra, here is a practical note from God's Word that lets you relax a bit—encouraging you to do something everyone enjoys: sleeping. It may seem like stating the obvious, but the reminder is important.

Lord, you know that some things keep me from sleeping.
Reveal to me reasons that I don't get enough sleep. Show
any discontentment I may have that causes me to overwork.
Take away my fears about my children and grandchildren,
and help me rest in your goodness and care for them.
Help me to sleep, Lord. Thank you for this quiet gift.

Sleep becomes hard work when we try to carry our burdens by ourselves.

30

Longing for Home

2 Timothy 4:6–8, 16–18

For I am already being poured out like a drink
offering, and the time for my departure is near.

2 Timothy 4:6

People who travel for ministry or business spend a lot of time away from home. Most likely, that means spending many, many nights in hotels, which often promise to make their visitors "feel at home." But that's not really possible. No matter how nice the accommodations, there's always that longing for home.

The apostle Paul had a deep longing for his heavenly home in his final days on earth. His thoughts turned toward heaven and the warm welcome he would receive from the Lord, "the righteous Judge" (2 Timothy 4:8). Although he was facing death, thoughts of heaven kept his spirit hopeful.

A man and his grandson were sitting on a dock one late afternoon. The two chatted about everything, it seemed: why water is wet, why seasons change, why girls hate worms, what life is like. Finally, the boy looked up and asked, "Grandpa, does anybody ever see God?" "Son," said the man as he looked across the still waters of the lake, "it's getting so now I hardly see anything else."

The passing of years should make us more like that. Praying should come more easily. Communion with the Father in heaven should be as natural as breathing. Thoughts of seeing Jesus and longing for our heavenly home should increasingly occupy our minds. That's how we'll know we're starting to get ready to go home.

You don't have to be elderly and standing on the edge of death to long for heaven. Your gratefulness to God for sending Jesus to redeem you can cause your mind to wonder about your eternal home. You know of those who are already there, and you can't help but try to imagine the glories He has prepared. Perhaps you can even influence your grandchildren to think about this amazing place.

Dear Father in heaven, thank you for your promise
of an eternal home with you. As I continue to
live on earth, it is so encouraging to know that
you have something better in store for me.

Being heavenly minded does us a world of earthly good.

31

Heaven's Silent Witness

Psalm 19:1–6

The heavens declare the glory of God; the skies proclaim the work of his hands.

Psalm 19:1

From the beginning of time, mankind has been amazed by the beauty and wonder of God's handiwork in the sky. The astounding clock of the heavens always keeps perfect time—with its intricate pattern of whirling spheres, glistening stars, and mysterious planets. Their majesty prompted the psalmist to praise the great Creator.

While tending his flocks, young David had ample time to gaze into the black velvet night that sparkled with the diamonds of God. As he looked, he delighted in the silent testimony that the heavens gave of their divine origin. He knew that the stars and the planets would continue to show forth God's reality and power. Do we have the same confidence David had? Does the wonder of the universe verify for us the power of God's mighty creation and lead us to praise His name?

During the French Revolution many leaders were determined to do away with Christianity. One clear night an atheist proclaimed his satanic doctrine to a countryman. "Everything," he ranted, "will be abolished—churches, Bibles, clergymen. Yes, even the word *God* itself! We will remove everything that speaks of religion." The listener gave a quiet chuckle. "Why do you laugh?" demanded the other. The man pointed to the stars and replied, "I was just wondering how you and your crew would manage to get them down!"

The glory of the heavens silently but undeniably testifies of God's existence.

Take your grandkids out to view the night sky. Talk with them about the God who is big enough to scatter planets and stars millions of miles into space. Talk about the fact that He created His majestic universe from nothing. And the fact that the earth is perfectly placed so life can exist and flourish. Then say a prayer of thanks.

Dear Lord, thank you that your heavens declare your glory and that your skies show me what your hands can do.

The heavens speak so loudly of God's handiwork that only the clamor of ignorance and sin causes some not to hear it.

32

The Secret of Long Life

Psalm 90

Teach us to number our days, that we
may gain a heart of wisdom.

Psalm 90:12

Recently, *Guinness World Records* said that the oldest woman alive is 118 and that she lives in France. *Parade* magazine once claimed that an American named Arthur Reed lived to be 123. The facts about Arthur were astounding. He married for the third time when he was 92, took five-mile walks when he was 100, and rode a bicycle until he was 110. According to the article, when he was asked the secret of a long life, he replied, "They made me of good dirt."

The writer of Psalm 90 suggests that anything beyond seventy is an exception to the rule. And no matter what kind of "good dirt" we are made of, our bodies will eventually go the way of the quickly fading flowers, the fleeting morning mists, and the dissipating clouds. Even the longest life—whether 118 or 123—eventually becomes like a quickly passing "day that has just gone by" before the everlasting God (Psalm 90:4). The psalmist wanted his readers to see how short our time on earth is compared to the length of eternity.

This reminder should cause us to ponder the secret of the life that is truly long—eternal life in heaven. It's to number our days, to use the time we have to prepare to live forever. It's to make sure of our salvation through faith in Christ and to live each day for Him.

Let's not miss life everlasting by assuming that even the oldest life gives us plenty of time to prepare for eternity. Today is the day of salvation.

Salvation in Jesus gives you the greatest promise ever: eternal life in God's presence. Imagine existing without God and His goodness! You can be grateful for the grand prospect of fellowship with a perfect God forever. Make sure you have received that free gift from God.

Dear Lord, I'm not sure I have ever trusted Jesus as my Savior. Today, I ask you to forgive my sins on the basis of your death on the cross to take my sins on yourself, and your resurrection to prove your power over death. Thank you for my salvation.

Eternity with Jesus in heaven will be infinitely better than even our best days here on earth.

33

Worship

2 Chronicles 7:1-11

When all the Israelites saw the fire coming down and
the glory of the Lord above the temple, they knelt
on the pavement with their faces to the ground,
and they worshiped and gave thanks to the Lord,
saying, "He is good; his love endures forever."

2 Chronicles 7:3

It wasn't a normal, run-of-the-mill morning worship service when Solomon dedicated the temple. There was the sacrifice of countless animals (2 Chronicles 5:6). Special music was provided by the Levites on stringed instruments, cymbals, and harps, and by 120 trumpet-playing priests (5:12). There was the thick cloud in which dwelt the glory of the Lord (5:14). There was the dedicatory prayer of Solomon (6:12–42).

The most dramatic event occurred, however, when fire fell from heaven and consumed the offerings (7:1). The people, awed by God's presence, bowed low in worship (7:3). Two weeks later, when Solomon sent them home, they were "joyful and glad in heart for the good things the Lord had done" (7:10).

Although we cannot duplicate the majesty of such a celebration, from it we can learn about the transforming power of worship. And we can be challenged as believers and as churches to seek to worship God more effectively.

Each time you attend church, review the mighty works God has done in your life and in the lives of your fellow worshipers. Bow before the Lord in gratitude for who He is, and sing praises to Him for His greatness, power, and glory. In the spirit of the people at the temple, let's joyfully worship the Lord.

You sometimes have to make a special effort to block out the distractions when you sing praises—the people around you, the crying child behind you, the musicians in front of you—and concentrate on God alone. When you do, worship can be truly joyful—between just one redeemed believer and God Himself.

Dear Lord, thank you for the element of worship
that you planned for our gatherings of believers, as
we have seen in Scripture. Help me to concentrate on
you and you alone each time I sing praises to you.

True, joyful worship unites us with the author
of our joy: our Savior Jesus.

34

How Can I Help?

1 Samuel 30:7–10, 21–25

Who will listen to what you say? The share of the man who stayed with the supplies is to be the same as that of him who went down to the battle. All will share alike.

1 Samuel 30:24

At the dedication ceremony of a cathedral in Milan, Italy, a little girl in the crowd cried out, "I helped build it. I helped build it!" "What!" exclaimed one of the guards. "Tell me what you did." The child replied, "I brought my daddy's lunch to him when he worked here."

She was right. Although she didn't take part in the construction, her efforts contributed to the completion of that beautiful edifice.

Heaven will be filled with many surprises. Among them, I think, will be the recognition given to believers who serve the Lord unknown and unappreciated. We can get the idea that the ones at the "front" in spiritual conflict with the Evil One will be more fully rewarded by the Lord than others. But all believers who faithfully fill God's place for them will hear the Savior say, "Well done."

In 1 Samuel 30:24, David said that those who remained behind with the supplies would share the spoils equally with those who fought the battle. The same is true in our service for Christ. Believers who do what they can—what God has equipped them to do—will be rewarded the same as those at the forefront. Jesus said that "the Son of Man is going to come in his Father's glory . . . , and then he will reward each person according to what they have done" (Matthew 16:27).

So, whether we are in the thick of the work of the Lord or helping behind the lines, there's a reward for all!

This is good news for all who have not been gifted to be up-front people. God cares as much for the person at church who prepares meals for the funeral as He does for the one who presides over the service. You could go on listing examples, but your comfort is in knowing that willing service, not the rank of the server, is important.

Lord, thank you for recognizing the work for you
that I do—even when I am behind the scenes. Help
all of your workers to feel the joy of your approval
as we seek to stand together for your glory.

Even the faithful prayers of an ailing senior saint
are a valuable service for the kingdom
and a key offering of service to God.

35

A Happy Life

Revelation 21:1–17

"He will wipe every tear from their eyes. There will be no more death" or mourning or crying or pain, for the old order of things has passed away.

Revelation 21:4

Cornelia Dobner was ninety when she died and went to her home in heaven. Her life had been characterized by hard work, self-sacrifice for her family, and loyalty to God and her husband.

Soon after the funeral, two of her great-granddaughters put their feelings into words by writing notes to her. One of them, in the clear block printing of a six-year-old, wrote, "I hope you have a happy life up in heaven."

That child's hope for her great-grandmother is an unquestioned certainty for every follower of Christ who dies. The Bible describes our eternal home as a place where there is no more suffering, sorrow, crying, pain, impurity, disease, or evil (Revelation 21:4, 27). It also tells us what is there: the Lamb (Jesus), the redeemed, the river of life, the throne of God, the tree of life, and the light of God (21:22; 22:1–5).

Jesus said that He would go to prepare a place for us (John 14:1–3). And the apostle Paul described it as the place where "we will be with the Lord forever" (1 Thessalonians 4:17). If that's not happiness, what is?

Yes, like Cornelia Dobner, every believer in Jesus can look forward to "a happy life up in heaven."

It's never too early to think seriously about some of the blessings that lie ahead in heaven for the believer in Jesus. And it's never too early to share those thoughts with your grandkids.

Dear Lord, I can't truly imagine what my future home in heaven will be like. But I know this: being with you will satisfy me forever. Help that truth to encourage me in this life as I influence others—especially my grandchildren—to have the assurance of going there too. Thank you for preparing that place for me.

A genuine anticipation of heaven is the joy and hope of every believer.

36

Puddles of Sunshine

John 1:1-5

The people living in darkness have seen a great light; on those living in the land of the shadow of death a light has dawned.

Matthew 4:16

I t was a warm summer day, and a grandpa and his four-year-old grand-daughter Mollie were taking a break from playing ball. As they sat on the porch with their glasses of water, Mollie looked out at the yard and said, "Look at the puddles of sunshine." The sunlight was filtering through the thick foliage to create a pattern of light amid the dark shadows formed by trees in the yard.

Puddles of sunshine. Isn't this a beautiful image for finding hope in dark days? In the midst of what can often be challenging times—when good news seems in short supply—instead of concentrating on the shadows, we can focus on the light.

The Light has a name—Jesus. Matthew quoted Isaiah to describe the brightness that came into the world when Jesus arrived: "The people living in darkness have seen a great light; on those living in the land of the shadow of death a light has dawned" (Matthew 4:16; see also Isaiah 9:2). The effects of sin are all around us as we live in the "land of the shadow of death." But shining through that shadow is Jesus, the grand and glorious light of the world (John 1:4–5).

The sunshine of Jesus's love and compassion breaks through the shadow, giving us "puddles of sunshine" to illuminate our day and brighten our hearts with hope.

How can you help your grandchildren see the light in a sometimes-dark world? How can you help them to avoid moving toward the darkness of sin that seems appealing to so many? Your example helps. Be the grateful, joyful, bright, and encouraging light that will draw them to you and the hope you see in Jesus.

Dear Lord, thank you for being the light of the world. And help me be the light of Jesus to my family. Amidst the shadows that sometimes gather around me, help me to be a beacon of sunshiny brightness that shines directly on Jesus.

The light of Jesus can illuminate any dark day or any shadow-filled life.

37

Knock, Knock

2 Timothy 1:8–12

Do not be ashamed of the testimony about our Lord.

2 Timothy 1:8

A knock came at the door of the home of a man with a young family. When the father answered the door, he was greeted by someone he had never met—a friendly man from a nearby church who had stopped by to say hello.

His pleasant demeanor and kind words impressed the dad, and the two agreed to meet again. When they did, the visitor introduced the father to the gospel of Jesus Christ. Both he and his wife trusted Jesus as Savior.

That changed everything. The couple began attending church, and all six of their children became believers in Christ. Eventually the dad became a Sunday school teacher and a deacon.

One of this couple's daughters grew up to attend a Christian college. There, she met a Christian guy she eventually married. Their family had four children, who grew up hearing the gospel. And those children would grow up to have families where Jesus was central to their lives. That door-to-door ambassador changed not just one man, but an entire family for generations—and the results continue to reverberate.

Paul encouraged us, "Let your speech always be with grace, seasoned with salt, that you may know how you ought to answer each one" (Colossians 4:6 NKJV).

Whose life, whose future, will you impact?

You don't know the results of your Jesus-oriented conversations. And actually, having those conversations leaves the work of salvation to the power of the Holy Spirit. But you can change lives and families by telling people about Jesus. The best way to show your gratitude for what Jesus has done for you is to tell someone about Him.

Lord, give me opportunities to use my words—however conveyed—to influence others about Jesus. Help me not to be "ashamed of the testimony" of Jesus Christ.

In a world of competing philosophies, only one message can make an eternal change: the gospel of Jesus.

38

Watcha Doin'?

Colossians 3:12-17

Be very careful, then, how you live—not as unwise but as wise.
Ephesians 5:15

While at her grandfather's house for a weeklong visit, little Addie began asking, "Whatcha doin', Grandpa?" over and over. Whether he was working at his computer, putting on his shoes to go outside, sitting down to read, or helping in the kitchen, she sidled up to him and asked him what he was doing.

After answering her a few dozen times with, "Paying bills," "Going to the store," "Reading a book," "Helping Grandma," he came to the conclusion that she was asking a key question.

Answering to a curious little girl about everything we do is one thing, he mused, but answering to God about our actions is infinitely more important. Wouldn't it be helpful to think of God coming alongside us at any time to ask, "What are you doing?" Imagine how often our answers would seem meaningless or empty.

"I'm spending the entire evening binge-watching a TV series." "I'm eating more food than I should." "I'm going another day without talking to you, Lord." "I'm arguing with my spouse." The list could go on—to our embarrassment.

Scripture suggests we use our time carefully—with God's glory in view (1 Corinthians 10:31; Colossians 3:23). Paul said, "Be very careful, then, how you live" (Ephesians 5:15). God wants to know: "Whatcha doin'?"

It's a double-edged sword (in a good way)—this concept that God wants to know what you are doing. First, it keeps you from doing what you know displeases Him. And second, it leads you to be doing something useful with your time. Praise God for this "pressure" on you. Out of your love for Him, that "pressure" becomes pleasure as you live for Him alone.

Dear Lord, guide my steps today. Whether I'm still working at a regular job or retired, I know I am still accountable to you for my time. Help me not to waste it.

A life well-lived consists of activities
that exercise the body, the mind, and the soul.

39

Special People

2 Samuel 9:1-13

Be like-minded, be sympathetic, love one
another; be compassionate and humble.

1 Peter 3:8

Hubert H. Humphrey (1911–1978), who served as a college professor, a senator, a US vice president, and a family man, spoke proudly and lovingly of his family in a television interview. Then his eyes moistened as he recalled the birth of Victoria, a very special granddaughter with Down syndrome. "It happened several years ago," he said at the time, "and do you know, that little girl has brought more love into our family circle than had existed before."

A few years later Humphrey died, and after the graveside service the family found it difficult to leave the cemetery. But it was Victoria who lifted their spirits. "Grandpa is in heaven, not in this casket," she said. What a blessing that little girl was to the Humphrey family before her death in 2010!

As king, David could have eliminated Saul's household for Saul's attempts to kill him. But he desired instead to show favor to any living member of Saul's family for his friend Jonathan's sake. When told about Mephibosheth, who was "lame in both feet" (2 Samuel 9:3), David showed him special kindness. His physical condition, as well as his place in Saul's household, brought out the best in David.

People with disabilities fulfill a unique place in God's plan. Let's learn from David's example.

No matter what disability you might have, you are "fearfully and wonderfully made" (Psalm 139:14). It is up to you to show kindness, fairness, love, compassion, and tenderness toward all—regardless of the physical situation. And if you have a grandchild with some form of disability, be grateful for him or her and surround that child with godly, unconditional love.

> *Dear God, the one who makes no mistakes, help me to love*
> *each grandchild the same, no matter the situation. Your*
> *love is boundless and perfect. Help me to mirror that love.*

**When God gives us children who are unique gifts
in special packages, care for them
and lavish them with love.**

40

Keep On Asking

Luke 11:1-13

So I say to you: Ask and it will be given to you.

Luke 11:9

A woman once bragged that she never prayed more than once for anything. She said she didn't want to weary God with her repeated requests.

The Lord's teaching on prayer in Luke 11 contradicts this notion. He told a parable about a man who went to his friend's house at midnight and asked for some bread to feed his unexpected visitors. At first the friend refused, for he and his family were in bed. Finally, the man got up and gave him the bread—not out of friendship but because the caller was so persistent (vv. 5–10).

Jesus used this parable to contrast this reluctant friend with our generous heavenly Father. If an irritated neighbor will give in to his friend's persistence and grant his request, how much more readily will our heavenly Father give us all we need!

It's true that God, in His great wisdom, may sometimes delay His answers to prayer. It's also true that we must pray in harmony with the Scriptures and God's will. But Jesus moved beyond those facts to urge us to persist in prayer. He told us to ask, seek, and knock until the answer comes (v. 9).

So don't worry about wearying God. He will never tire of your persistent prayers!

What a privilege God has given you in prayer. Even when you might feel helpless, you have a resource outside of yourself. Pray with persistence, knowing that God cares about all of your concerns.

*Dear Lord, thank you that you hear me right now—
and every time I pray. Help me to trust you and
depend on you. Help me not to be afraid to ask.*

The mystery of prayer is not the question
of whether God will do His part; the mystery
is why we don't pray more often.

41

Carried by Love

Isaiah 46:1–19

I have made you and I will carry you.
Isaiah 46:4

The four-year-old boy sat on his grandpa's lap and patted his bald head, studying it intently. "Papa," he asked, "what happened to your hair?" "Oh," he laughed, "I lost it over the years." The young boy's face turned thoughtful. "That's too bad," he responded. "I'll have to give you some of mine."

Grandpa smiled at his compassion and pulled him close for a hug. Reflecting later on his love for his grandson in that cherished moment also caused him to ponder God's selfless, generous love for this world.

G. K. Chesterton wrote: "We have sinned and grown old, and our Father is younger than we." By this he meant that the "Ancient of Days" (Daniel 7:9) is untainted by sin's decay—God is ageless, and He loves us exuberantly with a love that never falters or fades. He's totally willing and able to fulfill the promise He made to His people in Isaiah 46: "Even to your old age and gray hairs I am he, I am he who will sustain you. I have made you and I will carry you" (v. 4).

Five verses later He explains, "I am God, and there is none like me" (v. 9). The great "I AM" (Exodus 3:14) loves us so deeply that He went to the extreme of sending Jesus to die on the cross to bear the full weight of our sin. That love helps us know we should turn to Him in repentance and be free of our sin burden. Carried by His love, we gratefully worship Him forever!

The boy in the story, in his childlike wisdom, was willing to give up some of his hair for Grandpa. What are you willing to give up to show your love for your heavenly Father? Out of pure gratitude, eagerly worship and serve Him.

> *Thank you, Father, for your deep love for me. You shower me with good gifts both spiritually and physically, and I cannot thank you enough.*

The boundless love we have for our grandchildren is just a tiny picture of God's eternal and relentless love for those who put their trust in Him.

42

The Elijah Complex

1 Kings 19:1–8

[Elijah] came to a broom bush, sat down under
it and prayed that he might die. "I have had
enough, Lᴏʀᴅ," he said. "Take my life."

1 Kings 19:4

The concert is in full swing. The conductor is waving his baton with zeal and enthusiasm. Suddenly a member of the orchestra gets up and approaches him. It's the triangle player. He whispers, "Do you mind, sir, if I go home? I've come to the end of my part."

That's ridiculous, isn't it! As a member of the orchestra, he's expected to stay through the concert. His presence alone adds a touch that is needed for the orchestra to look complete. It would disturb and disrupt the others if musicians were to leave the moment they had finished their part.

Sometimes people who have passed certain age milestones feel like that triangle player. They believe they've fulfilled their purpose. Like Elijah, they yield to self-pity and wish God would take them home to heaven. Yet, whether they know it or not, they are still significantly adding to the "orchestra of life" by just being here. Many Christians have been encouraged by the patience, wisdom, and intercession of more seasoned people who love the Lord. These folks still have much to accomplish for God's glory—or He would not leave them here on earth.

Perhaps you sometimes feel your work is finished. Don't give in to the Elijah complex of self-pity. You're still here because you can have an influence on others. You can still make an impact!

In the orchestra of life, what instrument are you playing? You can be thankful that Scripture tells you that even the smallest task in the church is important—or you could say that the least important instrument still contributes to the song. Even if all you can do is to pray—that is vital. Just your existence, your presence, is important.

Lord, in my moments of retrospection, I recall when I felt that I had a bigger contribution to society or church or family. Help me not to dwell on what was but to concentrate on contributing to what is. Keep giving me that hopeful feeling of being where you want me to be.

Seeking God's purpose for your life is not just for young people; it's for every believer.

43

A Little Concern

Psalm 91:9–16

Keep your lives free from the love of money and be
content with what you have, because God has said,
"Never will I leave you; never will I forsake you."

Hebrews 13:5

D o you recall when you first heard you were going to be a grandparent? Did it cause you to have a bit of anxiety? Sure, we're not
supposed to worry, but if you begin to think about what kind
of world your grandchild will grow up in, you could be at least a little
concerned.

For instance, when this little child graduates from high school, what
will the world look like? How much will it cost to go to college? Will the
morals and ethics you so cherish be outmoded? And will the church still
be making an impact?

The future can be a scary place. The unknown can be overwhelming,
especially when the known has so many struggles of its own. That's why
we need to trust in God's promises.

No matter what situation our grandchildren will face or what trouble
the world will seem to be in, they can depend on God's promise of help.
God said, "Never will I leave you; never will I forsake you" (Hebrews
13:5). And Jesus said, "Surely I am with you always, to the very end of
the age" (Matthew 28:20).

Those are great promises to depend on when we start to worry about the future, whether it's our generation or the next one.

As you see changes swirl around you and realize how they affect your grandchildren, you can be grateful for Jesus's assurance that He will be with you always—and with your children's children.

Dear Father, I am concerned about my grandchildren.
Help me to do what I can to guide them toward you—and
then to trust in your almighty hand to protect them day
after day. Thank you for the assurances of your care.

Knowing that God will never forsake us gives us courage to flourish in a world that continues to change.

44

Time Off from God?

1 Chronicles 16:23–36

Sing to the Lord, all the earth; proclaim
his salvation day after day.

1 Chronicles 16:23

I t was Sunday afternoon, and all six members of the family were gathered around the table for dinner. As had become customary, four-year-old Bryson led off the pre-meal prayer. "Dear heavenly Father, thank you for this nice day," he said. "Thank you that we could go to church and Sunday school today." Then, to everyone's surprise, he said, "And we'll see you again next week."

What Bryson stated in his prayer is, to our detriment, how we often view the Christian life. We easily fall into a see-you-next-time attitude about God. We forget about Him as we fulfill our daily responsibilities. We go for days at a time trying to pay the bills, keep up with responsibilities, enjoy down time, and give attention to each family member. But we neglect to give God the time He deserves.

First Chronicles 16 sets forth some facts about God's power and majesty that should keep us thinking and talking about Him "day after day." We should "declare his glory" (v. 24). We should recognize His hand of creation in the heavens (v. 26). We should talk of the honor and majesty He commands, the strength He possesses, and the gladness He gives us (v. 27).

Each new day gives us new reasons to pray to God, to praise His name, and to proclaim His love. Let's make our worship of Him something we do "day after day." Let's see God every day. Not just on Sunday.

Sunday worship is indeed something to look forward to, and you can be grateful that God has given you the church. For many, it is the time of the week when they get the spiritual boost they need most. But thankfully the Christian life is a moment-by-moment thing. Think about at least one thing you can do each day to interact with the God who loves you.

Dear Lord, help me to make every day a little bit like Sunday. Help me to praise you, learn more about you, sing songs of worship to you, and fellowship with other believers in Jesus. Help me not to take time off from you.

When we trust Jesus as Savior, we give Him our life— not just our Sunday mornings.

45

A Good Reason

1 Timothy 5:1–9

But if a widow has children or grandchildren, these
should learn first of all to put their religion into practice
by caring for their own family and so repaying their
parents and grandparents, for this is pleasing to God.

1 Timothy 5:4

The two women occupied the aisle seats across from each other in the airplane. The flight was two hours, so a fellow flyer who sat nearby couldn't help but see some of their interactions. He could see that they knew each other—might even be related. He watched as the younger of the two (probably in her sixties) kept reaching in her bag to hand the older (perhaps in her nineties) fresh apple slices, homemade finger sandwiches, then a towelette for clean up, and finally a magazine to read. Each handoff was done with such tenderness, such dignity. As they stood to exit the plane, the observer told the younger woman, "I noticed the way you cared for her. It was beautiful." She replied, "She's my best friend. She's my mother."

Wouldn't it be great if we could all say something like that? Some parents are like best friends. Some parents are nothing like that. The truth is, those relationships are complicated at best. While Paul's letter to Timothy doesn't ignore that complexity, it still calls us to put our "religion into practice" by taking care of parents and grandparents—our "relatives," our "own family" (1 Timothy 5:4, 8).

We all too often practice such care only if family members were or are good to us. In other words, if they deserve it. But Paul offers up a more beautiful reason to repay them. Take care of them because "this is pleasing to God" (v. 4).

What better way to say "thank you" to a close relative than to treat that person with a Jesus kind of love—compassionate, tender, caring. Even if there has been estrangement, it's never too late to start taking the right steps.

Lord, I am so grateful for close relationships in my life—especially family members I can share life with. Help those relationships to grow and bear the fruit of Christian love and fellowship.

Family care is not earned; it is a natural part of the love God puts in our hearts.

46

Charlie's List

Psalm 119:1–8

Let the message of Christ dwell among you richly.
Colossians 3:16

When Charles Hayward died at the age of eighty-seven, he left a legacy for his children and grandchildren. He and his wife Virginia had faithfully served as missionaries for many years both in India and in South Africa. But at age seventy-three, he began to select and memorize portions of Scripture so he would "finish well" with his mind full of God's truth.

He called his project, "The Whole Bible Memorization Plan." His children call it, "Charlie's List." Charles chose a theme verse (Colossians 3:16), at least one verse from each Old Testament book, at least one from each New Testament narrative book, and a verse or verses from each chapter of the New Testament Epistles. He began with Genesis 15:6, "Abram believed the LORD, and he credited it to him as righteousness" and ended with Revelation 22:17, "Let the one who is thirsty come; and let the one who wishes take the free gift of the water of life."

All in all, Charles committed 239 verses to memory. He can remind us of the psalmist who wrote: "I learn your righteous laws" (Psalm 119:7) and "I have hidden your word in my heart that I might not sin against you" (v. 11). Like Charles, the psalmist meditated and delighted in God's Word (vv. 15–16). What better goal could any of us have than to fill our minds with God's truth.

Now, here's a challenge that could easily be dismissed: "I'm no good at memorizing." Nobody said you have to be good at it. Just try creating your own Charlie's List and see. Even if the memorizing doesn't come easily, becoming familiar with new passages will encourage you. You'll find yourself thanking God for new insights from His Word.

Dear Lord, I accept the challenge. Help me to memorize some verses at my own pace and for your glory. Then perhaps I can encourage others with what I learn by meeting this challenge.

Even after a lifetime of learning, there's still space in our minds for God's Word.

47

The Whole House

Acts 16:25-34

They replied, "Believe in the Lord Jesus, and you
will be saved—you and your household."

Acts 16:31

Although each of us inherited a sinful nature, which is transmitted by our parents, we do not inherit what we need the most: a saving relationship with our heavenly Father. But there is good news. God often brings about the salvation of an entire household.

A man attended a series of meetings in which the gospel was clearly explained. As he returned home, he decided to spend extra time praying for the salvation of his children. His wife and parents decided to join him in doing so.

One evening the teens in the family were planning to go off for an evening of partying—and this concerned their dad. Just before the kids left the house, the teens' grandmother—who lived with the family— asked to talk to them. She said, "Now, I want you to remember that while you are away, I am going to be praying the whole time for your salvation." And off they went to the party.

But all evening long, they were unable to forget what Grandma had told them. Their dad recalls that the next day someone was heard crying in an adjoining room. It was his daughter asking God to save her. Soon his son was praying to God for pardon and mercy. Before long the entire family was saved.

God wants to save all the members of your family. We should never stop praying for grandchildren to come to Jesus. Salvation is not inherited. But what a forceful influence the prayers of godly grandparents can be!

Grandparents who know Jesus can begin praying for their grandkids before they are born. And even if it seems they are headed down the wrong path, the prayers don't stop. What a privilege grandparents have!

Dear God, you know my grandchildren better than I do. You know what they need right now—whether it is salvation or encouragement along the path. Please guide them today.

Among the most important prayers we pray in our lifetime are our God-directed pleas to redeem other family members.

48

The Music of Heaven

Revelation 5

And they sang a new song, saying: "You are worthy
to take the scroll and to open its seals."

Revelation 5:9

A great celebration was staged in Boston in 1869 to commemorate the end of the American Civil War. A man who was there
wrote a letter to a friend and described some of the events.

He told of a 10,000-voice choir supported by a 1,000-piece orchestra.
The violin section included 200 musicians, led by the world's greatest
violinist, Ole Bull. A thousand anvils were used in the "Anvil Chorus."
And when the soloist sang "The Star-Spangled Banner" with the full
orchestra and chorus, her voice was so loud and clear that it seemed to
soar above everything else.

With those memories flooding his mind, the letter writer concluded,
"I am an old man now, but I am looking forward to the music of
heaven—music infinitely superior to the marvelous chorus I listened to
that day."

Yes, as thrilling as that music was, who can imagine the sound in
heaven when "thousands upon thousands, and ten thousand times ten
thousand" (Revelation 5:11) join in praise to our Lord!

All who love Jesus are looking forward to hearing the heavenly choirs
as they exalt Him. And we will each add our voice to theirs. Perhaps we

don't qualify to sing in any choir here on earth. But just wait till you hear what we sound like when we get there!

Of course, you don't like to think of leaving this world, but for just one moment transport yourself to the scene in heaven. Millions of people will sing praise to our great and awesome Savior—and you will sing unashamedly. The sound will be, well, heavenly. Enjoy that moment of anticipation, and praise God for the encouragement those thoughts give you.

Dear Father in heaven, thank you for singing. As I lift my voice in praise and worship now, I am seemingly practicing for heaven. Please accept my praise.

The sound of our voices in heaven, united in praise to God, is unimaginable.

49

The Tongue
of the Wise

Proverbs 12:13–25

The words of the reckless pierce like swords,
but the tongue of the wise brings healing.

Proverbs 12:18

You have probably heard the childish taunt, "Sticks and stones may break my bones, but words will never hurt me." And it may seem innocent enough. It's the kind of saying that grandmothers have been known to use when consoling their troubled grandchildren. One generation after another has picked it up and passed it along. But think about it. This piece of folk wisdom is questionable at best.

While sticks and stones can bring instant injury and pain, the results of words can be even worse. I'm reminded of this by a news story I read. Reportedly, an eight-year-old was detained by police for assaulting a playmate with a stick. But the real damage seemed to be done when the parents waged a war of words that carried the humiliation and embarrassment of the children onto the national stage through the press and social media.

Sticks and stones inflict injuries that usually pass. But words can go much deeper, sometimes causing pain that lasts a lifetime. Such words as, "I don't love you," "You're a failure," and "You're no good" can do permanent damage. The result? A person whose self-respect is so deeply wounded that he or she is unable to accept words such as, "I love you," "You're special," and "I appreciate you."

Proverbs 12:18 makes it clear that we must watch our words. "The words of the reckless pierce like swords, but the tongue of the wise brings healing." This should be our daily prayer as we interact with others: "May these words of my mouth and this meditation of my heart be pleasing in your sight, LORD" (Psalm 19:14).

A grateful heart—one that understands God's graciousness to you—is one that guides you to speak gracious words to others. That idea can help you remember to offer words of kindness and encouragement to your grandchildren.

Lord, guard my words, and help them to flow from a heart of love and gratitude. Help me to demonstrate to my family the power of kind words.

Taking a few seconds to weigh our words before we say them can relieve others of a heavy burden.

50

"It Always Comes to That"

2 Kings 19:14-19

Hezekiah received the letter from the messengers and read it. Then he went up to the temple of the LORD and spread it out before the LORD.

2 Kings 19:14

The Northern Kingdom of Israel had been carried into captivity by the Assyrians. Another invading army had marched south and had taken the fortified cities of Judah. Now the enemy was encamped outside of Jerusalem. When King Hezekiah was told of this, he went immediately to the house of the Lord and prayed. His response helps us see a vital principle of godly living: When facing a crisis, we must go to God at once and trust Him for the outcome.

A beloved grandmother was greatly disturbed by her many troubles—both real and imaginary. Finally, someone in her family tactfully told her, "Grandma, we're doing all we can to help you. You'll just have to trust God for the rest." A look of despair spread over her face as she replied, "Oh dear, has it come to that?"

It always comes to that, doesn't it? So why don't we begin with that? God's Word tells us to bring every concern to the Lord (1 Peter 5:7). He offers to take our problems on His shoulders, so why not let Him?

Sometimes we're like that grandmother. We think of God as a last resort. We struggle with our problems and work ourselves into a state of worry. A better course is to remember that our heavenly Father wants to help us. In fact, He is glorified when we go to Him at once.

You honor the Lord and His greatness when you start by letting Him know right away what is bothering you. (Spoiler alert: He already knows about it.) It's more exciting to do what you need to do about a problem while trusting Him. Then you can be amazed at how He works.

Dear Lord, I know you don't want me to be passive or lazy about things, but you also don't want me to try to take everything on by myself. Teach me the balance of using the skills and assets you've given me while leaning on you for help.

**If you have a burden, go to God.
It always comes to that, so why not begin with that!**

51

Plenty to Do

Proverbs 16:31

Teach the older men to be temperate, worthy of respect,
self-controlled, and sound in faith, in love and in endurance.

Titus 2:2-3

What do the retirement years offer? Well, one man who had already arrived at that stage of life said, "The job of the retiree is learning to live as a nobody. You're a vice president of nothing."

Is this true? Can the golden years of a person's life be that bad? Apparently, they are for some people. For instance, doctors and therapists report that alcoholism can turn into a problem with many retired folks. Those medical professionals conclude that these drinkers have too much time and unchanneled energy, so they feel useless. Some retirees feel that the only thing that remains for them is losing their health, their mate, and life itself.

But wait. Enough of this gloom! That's not the right way to look at things. The Christian who reaches the retirement years does not have to be overwhelmed by feelings of anxiety and uselessness. God has a purpose for His people of all ages. Proverbs 16:31 tells us that "gray hair is a crown of splendor." And Titus 2:1–5 makes it clear that seasoned believers are to maintain a good example. They are to be teachers and models of righteousness for the younger generation. The Christian must continue giving time and energy to God and to neighbors. We find true worth in the gratifying work and company of the Lord Himself.

As you think about the years of grandparenting and retirement, look ahead to the purposes God has for you as you walk with Him each day of your life.

Some people say that since they retired, they are so busy that they can't imagine how they used to have time to go to their job. Being overly busy isn't a top priority, but finding ways to continue serving God is. Think of five ways you can stay active as a way of saying thanks to God for His continued faithfulness.

Dear Lord, this stage of life, like every other time in the years you have given me, is valuable! Thank you for each day and each way I can stay focused on service to you and others.

Behind are the memories; ahead is the adventure. Don't dwell on the memories without looking for the adventure.

52

It's Late

Titus 2:11–15

Dear children, this is the last hour.

1 John 2:18

Ayoung boy was playing in his grandmother's house near a large grandfather clock. Noontime was approaching, and when both hands of the old timepiece reached twelve, the chimes began to ring.

As he always liked to do, the boy counted each gong as it sounded. This time, however, something went wrong with the clock's inner mechanism. Instead of stopping at twelve, it kept right on chiming—thirteen, fourteen, fifteen, sixteen times.

The boy couldn't believe his ears! He jumped to his feet and ran into the kitchen, shouting, "Grandma! Grandma! It's later than it's ever been before!"

In his excitement, the youngster expressed a truth we all would do well to consider. It is later than it's ever been before—in the history of the world, in the days allotted to man, and on God's calendar of events. With each passing hour, the words of James 5:8 take on added significance: "The Lord's coming is near."

This fact is both comforting and sobering. It's reassuring to know that the day our Savior will come for us may be near. But at the same time, we must honestly ask ourselves, "Am I living in a way that will bring His commendation?"

Remember, "It's later than it's ever been before!"

How does the imminent return of the Lord Jesus change your thinking about day-to-day activities? Or how does it make you rethink your concern about family members who don't know Jesus? Your anticipation of the culmination of God's plan is a good way to say "thank you" to Him.

Dear heavenly Father, I so look forward to being with you, and I trust your timing for your return. Help me to both look forward to that and stay active for you while I wait.

We don't know how many days God will give us, so let's use each day for His honor and glory.

53

Legacy of Love

1 Thessalonians 2:17–3:13

May the Lord make your love increase and overflow for each other and for everyone else, just as ours does for you.

1 Thessalonians 3:12

What happens when a ten-year-old girl ties a note to a helium-filled balloon and sends it on its way to heaven? According to syndicated columnist Bob Greene, a grieving Illinois girl named Sarah sent such a letter to her grandfather, who had died before she could have one last visit with him. The letter was addressed to "Grandpa Bernie, in Heaven Up High." It represented a little girl's expression of love—and her hope that somehow Grandpa would hear.

Two months passed, and then a letter arrived addressed to Sarah. It began, "Your letter to Grandpa Bernie apparently reached its destination and was read by him. I understand they can't keep material things up there, so it drifted back to Earth. They just keep thoughts, memories, love, and things like that."

If we are moved by this girl's love for her grandpa, what about those we love who are still living? Death and eternity have a way of putting things in perspective.

Paul, in his first letter to the Thessalonians, wrote as one who knew the lasting value of relationships. He expressed his deep love and encouraged the people in Thessalonica to increase in their love for one another (3:12).

People, their faith, and their love are what count. Leaving a legacy of love is the best way to avoid having nothing left but wishful longings.

Is there someone who needs to hear from you—maybe even someone from many years ago? Someone who needs to know that you love them and care? Leaving a legacy of love is a sign of gratitude to the One who loved us before we loved Him.

Dear Lord, I wonder what my legacy is to people who know me best. Is it one of love or of indifference? Guide me. Help my love for others to increase and overflow.

No bucket list is complete without this goal: to love my family and other people with godly devotion.

54

The Power of Service

John 13:2–20

Christ Jesus . . . made himself nothing by
taking the very nature of a servant.

Philippians 2:5, 7

Money is power." That principle drives most cultures of the world. People scramble for wealth, often at the price of personal integrity, in order to gain the power to live where and how they want, drive the kind of vehicle they want, and get whatever else they want.

In a culture that worships money, believers in Jesus Christ are in danger of doing the same. Some use their money to control their family, or they may threaten to stop giving to their church if they don't get their way.

How unlike Jesus! He had power over disease, and He used it to heal the sick. He had power over the sea, and He used it to remove fear. He had power to create, and He fed thousands. He had power over sin, and He forgave sinners. He had power over His own life, yet He willingly gave it up to save all who would call upon Him (Romans 10:13).

Jesus possessed all power, but He used it to serve others. He was called "Lord" by the disciples in the upper room, yet He was the only servant there (John 13:2–17). He washed their feet! When Peter protested, Jesus answered, "Unless I wash you, you have no part with me" (v. 8).

Instead of using money or anything else for selfish means, use it to serve others. That's the right use of power.

Grandchildren learn many things from their grandparents, and one of the best things they can learn as they watch you is an attitude of servanthood. Through your godly use of money and time, you show them that you seek only to point people to Jesus. Think about your recent interactions with them. Did they see this in you?

Dear Lord, it's sometimes hard to have the attitude of Jesus—the true servanthood He displayed. Help me to put myself aside and think of Him as I deal with my grandchildren.

A Christian uses their power to serve others selflessly.

55

Tell the Children

Psalm 78:1–8

We will tell the next generation the
praiseworthy deeds of the LORD.

Psalm 78:4

Imagine an evening in ancient Israel. The day's work is done, the meal is finished, and the family is gathered around a small fire that pushes away the night chill and casts a soft glow on their faces. It's story time.

Father and grandfather take turns relating to the children the "praiseworthy deeds of the LORD" (Psalm 78:4). They tell of Abraham's journey. They speak of Isaac. Their voices come alive when they talk about old Jacob. They remember Moses and Joshua and Elijah and the great King David. They recount the history of their own family. And all the time they focus their attention on the mighty works of God on behalf of His people.

That's the way Jewish men fulfilled their responsibility to tell the next generation about the Lord. They had been told by their parents, who had been told by their parents.

Our children and grandchildren need to know about God. They need to learn from us about His love, His faithfulness, and His grace. They need to hear from us about the times He stepped into our lives to protect and provide.

So, gather up your sons and daughters and grandchildren. Relate to them how God has worked in your life. Fulfill your responsibility. Tell the children.

What an example set by the Jewish fathers of Old Testament days! You can add to their stories of Jewish patriarchs the stories of New Testament followers of Jesus and of people today who are making a difference for Jesus. Thankful for such amazing stories to tell, you can offer stories of faith to a new generation.

Dear Lord, thank you for those who told me of God's truth, and help me to pass along the stories to the children of my family. Help me to find the right time and the right way to share God's stories.

Grandmothers and grandfathers tell great stories!
And those stories get even better
when they include God's story.

56

Spring Beauty

Isaiah 40:1–8

The grass withers and the flowers fall, but
the word of our God endures forever.

Isaiah 40:8

As a grandpa and his nine-year-old granddaughter, Kelsey, took a springtime stroll through the woods together, she taught him something about plants. He hadn't noticed, until Kelsey pointed it out, that the forest floor was painted light pink with thousands of tiny flowers. "Those are spring beauties," she informed him. She went on to show him dogtooth violets, Dutchman's-breeches, and trillium.

After Kelsey called his attention to the wildflowers, he began to see them everywhere. He began to notice what delicate beauty they brought to the landscape! And he was amazed and delighted with the natural beauty he and his granddaughter could share.

Later, he told her, "If we come back in a week or so, these flowers will be all gone. They're beautiful, but they last only a short time. We'll have to wait till next year to see them again." But Kelsey said she already knew that. She had studied the seasons in school.

What Kelsey may not have known, though, is what wildflowers can teach us about the Bible. The flowers last a few days and are gone, Isaiah told us, but the Word of God lasts forever (40:8).

God's Word isn't just a spring beauty. It never fades, dries up, or blows away. Its treasures are there for us to appreciate each day.

Have you taken a walk through God's Word lately? Did you catch the beauty and majesty there?

The beauty of the world around you is astounding. You see it in flowers and sunsets and majestic mountains. You stand in grateful awe at their beauty. What is it about God's Word that is beautiful to you? How does it draw out your gratitude to God?

Creator God, I cannot stop being amazed by the beauty of what you have created, yet I know everything is temporary except for your eternal Word. Renew my wonder at what it reveals about the gospel and eternity with you.

The words of Scripture hold a beauty unrivaled even in the majesty of a forest filled with wildflowers.

57

He's Near to Hear

Psalm 145:17–21

The Lord is near to all who call on him,
to all who call on him in truth.

Psalm 145:18

When the little boy was seven, his grandfather was caretaker of a wooded estate. One fall evening the first grader took his toy gun, called for his dog Pal, and headed down a path into the forest. He walked bravely into the woods. Soon, though, it began to get dark, and he panicked. "Grandpa!" he shouted, hoping to shout loud enough for his grandfather to hear him back at the house.

"I'm right here," he replied, for he was only a few yards away. He had seen his grandson go into the woods and had followed him to make sure he was okay. The little boy was surprised and relieved!

As followers of Christ, we sometimes venture into unfamiliar territory. We try new things. We take on responsibilities in the work of the Lord that are bigger than we ever attempted before. We risk rejection when we talk to friends about Christ. It can get pretty scary.

But wherever we go, God is there with us. His pledge to be near us is backed up by His omnipresence. And His promise to help us is backed up by His mighty power. He will hear the cries of those who fear Him (Psalm 145:19–20).

So, take some risks in your walk with God. Venture out into the scary unknown in serving or giving or sharing your faith. God is nearer to you than Grandpa was to that adventurous boy in the darkening woods. He will always hear your cry.

Venturing into a new stage of life can be frightening—grandparenting, moving into a new home, changes in work status, retirement. Yet you have the assurance of God's closeness. What venture is standing in front of you? How can you plan now to have confidence in God's nearness?

Dear Lord, even at this stage of life, new challenges await. Please stay close as I try new things or seek new challenges. Help me to sense your nearness when things seem a bit different or even frightening.

What seem like fearful steps of faith into new areas of life or service are never solo ventures.

58

Cutting a Trail

Proverbs 4:1–7

Listen, my sons, to a father's instruction; pay
attention and gain understanding.

Proverbs 4:1

The Native Americans of Michigan were the state's first highway route engineers. With few exceptions, Michigan's major highways follow the trails they cut through the wilderness hundreds of years ago. A trail was twelve to eighteen inches wide, and for safety the people followed single file. Later, pack horses followed these trails, widening them. Then came wagons, and the trails became dirt roads. And now they are busy highways.

In a similar way, Solomon followed the trail of his father and in turn paved the way for his sons and grandsons. He did this by encouraging his sons to heed his instructions just as he had followed the sound teaching of his father (Proverbs 4:4–5). So, this father, while giving his sons good practical and spiritual counsel, was passing on what he had learned from the boys' grandfather, David, who was called a "man after [God's] own heart" (1 Samuel 13:14; Acts 13:22). The younger generation of believers often learns about God best from family.

Our physical and spiritual children watch the path we're taking. As God's men and women, let's make certain we cut a righteous, wise, and clear trail. Then if ongoing generations choose to follow, the trail can become a highway—an ongoing legacy to God's glory.

Think of those who paved the way for you to come to faith in Jesus. And, in gratitude for that great gift through them, seek ways to extend that highway—clearing the way for future generations to trust Jesus.

Dear God, may this analogy of cutting a trail help me to see how important it is to create a pathway to Jesus for any of my grandkids who don't know Him. Give me wisdom, Lord, to find the actions and words that can help them want to know about what Jesus has done for them.

When the path we take leads to Jesus, it may become a highway of faithfulness for future family followers.

59

God Is There

Genesis 28:10–15, 20–22

If God will be with me and will watch over
me . . . , then the Lord will be my God.

Genesis 28:20–21

Aubrey bought a fleece-lined coat for her aging father, but he died before he could wear it. So, she tucked a note of encouragement along with a $20 bill into the pocket and donated the jacket to charity.

Ninety miles away, unable to endure his family's dysfunction any longer, nineteen-year-old Kelly left his house without grabbing a coat. He knew of only one place to turn—the home of his grandmother who prayed for him. Hours later he stepped off a bus and into his grandma's arms. Shielding him from the winter wind, she said, "We've got to get you a coat!" At the mission store, Kelly tried on a coat he liked. Slipping his hands into the pockets he found an envelope—with a $20 bill and Aubrey's note.

Jacob fled his dysfunctional family in fear for his life (Genesis 27:41–45). When he stopped for the night, God revealed himself to Jacob in a dream. "I am with you and will watch over you wherever you go," God told him (28:15). Jacob vowed, "If God will . . . give me food to eat and clothes to wear . . . , then the Lord will be my God" (vv. 20–21).

Jacob made a rudimentary altar and named the spot "God's house" (v. 22). Kelly takes Aubrey's note and that $20 wherever he goes. Each serves as a reminder that no matter where we run, God is there.

The life you have lived can be a testimony to your grandchildren. Remind them how thankful you are that God was with you when you were in school. When you were in the military. When you worked at your first job. When you were battling illness. Whatever your situation was. Share those times. Tell the children that God never abandoned you—and He won't abandon you. And then ask them to tell you the situations where they need that reminder.

Dear Lord, I still need your presence—and sometimes I forget that you are here. Help me to remember that you are near me during the difficult times and the good times.

God's presence is like the air we breathe; we can't see it, but we know it is there because it keeps us alive.

60

The Value of a Child

Mark 9:33–37

> Whoever welcomes one of these little
> children in my name welcomes me.
>
> Mark 9:37

The young girl lived halfway around the world in war-ravaged Cambodia. She had been abandoned to the streets, destined to a life of much poverty and little love.

That was before Paul and Linda heard about her and sought to adopt her. "We did a lot of praying," Paul told a newspaper reporter.

For more than two years, the family dedicated themselves to bringing this girl, whom they named Caitlin, to their home in the US. They filled out mountains of paperwork. They even took one hopeful trip to Cambodia, only to come back empty-handed. But they kept praying.

A couple of years later, Paul took another trip, spending several frustrating weeks trying to gain custody of Caitlin. Finally, Linda got a phone call from Paul. He asked, "Guess who I have with me?" and his family erupted in cheers. Dad and daughter arrived home on Christmas Eve.

What a reminder of the pricelessness of a child! Each one is worth whatever it takes to care for him or her properly. Whether the child is a member of our family or a child we don't know—each is precious to God. Each needs love. Each needs to learn about Jesus, the One who by words and example taught us the value of a child (Mark 9:36–37).

No matter how many grandchildren you have—or how they came into your family—they are priceless. Take some time to thank God for each of them, and show each one how special he or she is to you.

Lord, I cannot express enough how grateful I am to you for my grandchildren. The value of a grandchild has no bounds, and you are so gracious to bring each grandchild into my family. Help me to show each grandchild you give me how special he or she is.

What a grand creation is each little child!
And what a privilege it is to protect and nurture
each one for God's appointed purpose in their lives.

61

Little Big Jobs

John 4:1-8, 27-38

"My food," said Jesus, "is to do the will of him
who sent me and to finish his work."

John 4:34

I s our work for the Lord really all that important in today's world?
When set against the activities of society's "movers and shakers,"
teaching a Sunday school class, for instance, looks like child's play.
But not in God's eyes. Whatever we do to advance His kingdom in this
world is the most important business of all.

D. J. De Pree (1891–1990) felt this keenly. For many years he headed
up a large corporation that produces office furniture. After retirement, he
taught a Sunday school class until his declining strength forced him to
give it up at age ninety-eight. When a class member visited him in the hospital, Mr. De Pree said, "It was harder for me to resign my Sunday school
class than to step down from being president of the furniture company."

When Jesus discussed spiritual issues with the Samaritan woman, He
was doing His Father's work (John 4:32–38). And it strengthened His
spirit just as food nourishes the body. Why? Because He was doing eternal work.

So, whether you teach Sunday school, do other tasks in the church,
or work your daily job, never forget that you are doing eternal work. No
need to envy people with "big" jobs. Serving Christ in the smallest way
is the biggest job you can do on earth.

You never have to feel that the job God gave you in life was small. Whether you ran a stamping machine, worked as a seamstress, sold RVs, or superintended a school system, you can be thankful that God put you in a place of influence on others. Those days at work—whether in the past or ongoing—are days of service for God. They give you a chance to honor God with your abilities and have an influence for Jesus on your coworkers.

> *God, thank you for work. You ordained work, and you use it for your honor. Thank you for allowing me to _____ while also demonstrating godliness and diligence. As a grandparent, help me influence my grandkids to see work that way as well.*

No job assigned and blessed by an almighty God can be considered small.

62

Home at Last

1 Corinthians 4:1–5

Judge nothing before the appointed time; wait until
the Lord comes. He will bring to light what is hidden in
darkness and will expose the motives of the heart. At
that time each will receive their praise from God.

1 Corinthians 4:5

Many years ago, a veteran missionary couple who had served God
for fifty years in a remote African village returned to the United
States for a well-earned retirement. When they arrived, however,
no one was there to greet them because of some confusion at the mission
office. They had no one to help them with their suitcases and trunks, and
no one to move them into their home. The man complained to his wife,
"We've come home after all these years, and there's no one who cares."

The man's bitterness grew as they settled into their new home. His wife,
a bit fed up with his complaining, suggested that he take up the matter
with God. So the man went to his bedroom and spent time in prayer.
When he came out, he had a new look on his face, which prompted his
wife to ask what had happened.

"Well," he replied, "I told God that I've come home, and no one cares."

"And what did God say?" she asked.

"He said, 'You're not home yet.'"

It is easy to think that our long years of service and faithfulness have
attracted no one's attention. All those years of teaching school. Or

being a good parent. Or fixing cars. Or serving at church. Did anyone see it?

God did, and He cares more than you can imagine. One day, when we reach our eternal home, "each will receive their praise from God" (1 Corinthians 4:5). In the meantime, let's stick to what He has called us to do (v. 2).

In your dark moments of self-regret, you can feel like that retired missionary. But then you read 1 Corinthians 4:5 and have a renewed attitude. Imagine what it will be like to "receive praise" from God for everything you've done for Him.

> *Father in heaven, I cannot even begin to comprehend what it will be like to hear "Well done" from you. Keep me thinking of new ways to serve you—even if at times I feel unappreciated. Because I know you know!*

If you are looking around for someone to notice the good things you are doing for God's glory, look up.

63

"It's Pretty Exciting"

Psalm 71

Do not cast me away when I am old; do not
forsake me when my strength is gone.

Psalm 71:9

Two friends—one of whom had just celebrated his sixtieth birthday—went out for breakfast together. They discussed the "trauma" of the number six being the first digit in someone's age and everything that the age of sixty might imply (retirement, social security, etc.). They also pondered the fact that the "birthday boy" felt so much younger than such a "large" number would seem to indicate.

Then the conversation turned to the lessons, joys, and blessings he had found in living those sixty years, and he said, "You know, it isn't really that bad. In fact, it's pretty exciting." The lessons of the past had brought a change in how he viewed the present.

Such is the process of putting years on life's calendar. We learn from our past in order to live in our present—a lesson reflected on by the psalmist: "For you have been my hope, Sovereign LORD, my confidence since my youth" (Psalm 71:5). He continued, "From birth I have relied on you; you brought me forth from my mother's womb. I will ever praise you" (v. 6). As the psalmist looked back, he clearly saw the faithfulness of God. With confidence in that faithfulness, he could face the future and its uncertainties—and so can we.

May we say with the psalmist, "I will praise you . . . for your faithfulness, my God" (v. 22).

No matter which side of sixty you live on, there is so much to thank God for. Take a few moments to list some of the many blessings God has allowed you to enjoy. And don't leave out the hard parts—there are lessons and blessings there too.

Dear Lord, I can't say it any better than the psalm writer:
"I will praise you for your faithfulness." Help me to
make a habit of seeing the long life you have given me
as a blessing, despite the difficulties aging can bring.

> **The greater our appreciation for God's role in our life,**
> **the more grateful we'll be for how long He's allowed us**
> **to enjoy that life.**

64

Fiber Man

Psalm 1

In His law he meditates day and night. He shall
be like a tree planted by the rivers of water.

Psalm 1:2–3 NKJV

D r. Denis Burkitt achieved fame for discovering the cause and cure
of a disease named after him—Burkitt's lymphoma. He also received widespread acclaim for demonstrating the benefits of a
fiber-rich diet, which earned him the amusing nickname "Fiber Man."

What many people don't know, however, is that Dr. Burkitt was not
merely a great medical pioneer; he was a dedicated servant of God who
daily spent much time in prayer and meditation on God's Word. He
observed, "I am convinced that a downgrading in priority of . . . prayer
and biblical meditation is a major cause of weakness in many Christian communities. . . . Bible study demands pondering deeply on a short
passage, like a cow chewing her cud. It is better to read a little and ponder a lot than to read a lot and ponder a little."

Dr. Burkitt didn't leave just a great legacy of healing; he left an example of personal holiness and closeness with the Lord. The secret was
his lifelong habit of setting aside a specific time for prayer and reflection
on God's Word.

Few of us will ever enjoy accomplishments like his, but by following
the prescription of Psalm 1 we can attain the same spiritual health that
he did.

Who do you know in your circle of friends who appears to be in the Word and in prayer every day? What an influence that can be as it challenges you to have that same kind of diligence and dedication. And these habits can influence others—grandchildren included. A dedicated time with God demonstrates a true sense of thankfulness for what He has done and what His Word can teach you.

Lord, help me to be daily dedicated to prayer and reading and meditating on Scripture. I know you want to hear from me, and I know you have much to say in your Word to me. Help me to listen and learn.

Maintaining good health—physically and spiritually— is never effortless.

65

On Creaky Knees

Psalm 116

Because he turned his ear to me, I will
call on him as long as I live.

Psalm 116:2

Meet Margaret the battler. More than ninety years of memories and faith were her legacy, but she was not ready to surrender. Her life was full of the physical pain that often accompanies old age, and even though she was too weak to walk anymore, Margaret was not done with her ministry.

Despite her increasing feebleness, and despite her near deafness and inability to move around, Margaret had a ministry that reached far beyond the walls of the nursing home where she lived. Every day—often for hours at a time—she would sit in her chair with a stack of prayer cards and pray diligently for missionaries. And sometimes, when she could push her frail body to do so, she would kneel beside her bed on creaky knees to talk with God.

Margaret didn't have much more than prayer to offer her Lord. She was the essence of the answer to the question in Psalm 116:12, "What shall I return to the LORD for all his goodness to me?" Verse 13 answers, "I will . . . call on the name of the LORD."

A lifetime of being sustained by God's love, grace, and mercy finally ended for Margaret. But before her body finally gave out, she stayed spiritually strong to the end. Oh to have her courage and dedication—at any age!

How grateful you can be for warriors like Margaret! What is it that drives them to such dedication? It must be an intense and unfailing love for Jesus, for only by His Spirit could anyone soldier on as Margaret did. As you grow more in your love for your Savior, you too can redouble your efforts to intercede for others.

Dear Lord, I have other things I must do in my daily life besides pray. Yet you said to pray continually. Help me to be in an attitude of prayer so that even in the midst of must-be-done chores and activities, I am in communication with you.

Prayer warriors needed. No age limit!

66

A Better Attitude

Deuteronomy 32:44–52

Take to heart all the words I have solemnly declared
to you this day, so that you may command your
children to obey carefully all the words of this law.

Deuteronomy 32:46

Good news! Science and medicine are placing a great emphasis on living longer and better. Despite this, we can't avoid growing old. Aging will eventually overtake all of us.

But wait. Don't despair. Beyond science and medicine there is some good news! We can avoid succumbing to an attitude of bitterness and regret as we edge upward on life's calendar.

Look at the life of Moses. When he was 120 years old, he stood with the Israelites before they crossed the Jordan River and entered the Promised Land. He could not go with them because he had disobeyed the Lord when in anger he struck the rock in the wilderness (Numbers 20:12, 24).

How easily Moses could have slipped into a self-pitying and resentful frame of mind! Had he not faithfully and wisely borne the burden of a stubborn and stiff-necked people for forty years? Had he not interceded for them time after time? But for hitting a rock, he was banned from the Promised Land!

Yet at the end of his life, he praised the Lord and urged a new generation of Israelites to obey Him (Deuteronomy 32:1–4, 45–47).

As we grow older, we have a choice: Dwell on the failures and hardships of our past or recall God's faithfulness, accept His instruction, and keep looking to the future in faith. Leaning into and obeying God is the only way to have a better attitude—not a bitter one.

What is something you regret doing that still haunts you? Try what Moses did. Praise God for His forgiveness (1 John 1:9 helps) and redirect your thinking to ways to encourage those who are following behind. Then instead of grief, you'll have gratitude.

> *Dear Lord, thank you for Moses's example. Help*
> *me to look past my failures and see the resurrected*
> *Jesus. Help me to serve Him and point the people*
> *following behind me to Him and Him alone.*

As they say, age is a matter of mind over matter.
If you don't mind, it doesn't matter.

67

Get into the Habit

Psalm 55:16–23

Three times a day [Daniel] got down on his knees
and prayed . . . , just as he had done before.

Daniel 6:10

The family car is packed to the limit. The kids have their books, videos, and devices. The stacked bags in the back of the SUV clearly signal to all observers that the family is taking a trip. But before they leave the driveway, they stop and pray—asking God for safety and for family unity on the trip. It's a family habit.

Prayer habits are helpful tools to remind us of our dependence on God. Perhaps you have some habits of your own. Before you eat, you pray. Maybe before your grandkids head back home after a short stay at your house, you pray. Before they go to bed during sleepovers, you pray.

Developing prayer habits can be of tremendous help to those of us who want to enhance our relationship with the Lord but find that the routines of the day squeeze out prayer time. When we designate different activities of the day before or after which we always pray, we'll help to assure ourselves of regular communication with our Creator. That could become empty ritual, but it doesn't have to be—it can be a time of rich fellowship with our Lord.

David, who wrote Psalm 55, said that he prayed in the morning, noon, and evening (v. 17). Daniel prayed three times a day (Daniel 6:10). Like them, we would be wise to develop prayer habits. They're great ways to make prayer an integral, constant part of our daily lives—and a great example for those children and young people who call us their grandparents.

Clearly, prayer is not just asking for things from God, even though that is part of it. It is also saying thanks for the countless blessings He pours out. Perhaps begin a list of continual prayer requests, and add another list of things for which you can be grateful.

Dear Lord, help me make praying a daily habit—a continual attitude of thinking about you and talking to you.

A daily calendar that doesn't have a slot for prayer needs to be revised.

68

Say It!

Song of Songs 2:10-14

My beloved spoke and said to me, "Arise, my
darling, my beautiful one, come with me."

Song of Songs 2:10

I t's easy to take for granted the ones we love. Perhaps we get caught up in the day-to-day processes of living and working, and we neglect to share our true inner feelings. "She knows I love her," we tell ourselves. But we suddenly realize that it's been a couple of weeks since we've said "I love you" to our spouse.

Maybe you grew up in a family where positive, loving feelings were never expressed in words, so you still aren't comfortable doing that. Perhaps you're afraid you'll say the wrong thing or that if you try to express your feelings you won't be able to control them. That's okay, even if you cry.

An old ad slogan that began over a hundred years ago yet is still used today says, "Say it with flowers!" Maybe that's how you tell that special someone of your love. Or perhaps you say it with a well-chosen card. One man whose wife loves dark chocolate gives her candy and a card on special occasions. She told him she appreciates these tokens of love, but he has learned not to let the card or the gift do all the work. He realizes that he needs to say the words "I love you."

Everyone needs to hear words of love—from your spouse to your children (even if they are adults) to your grandchildren.

Today, tell that special person "I love you," not just with candy or flowers but with true, heartfelt words.

Take a little inventory of your conversations with those you love. Keep track over a period of time to see how often you tell them you love them. Perhaps if it's not happening enough, look for ways to do so. Maybe at the end of a phone conversation with a grandchild, sneak in an "I love you." Your heart will be filled with gratitude when you hear a return "I love you" from him or her.

Dear Lord, now that I think about it, I don't say "I love you" to you often enough. But I really do love you because of who you are and because of your love for me. Help me to give this important little message to my family members the next time I talk with them.

> Acts of love combined with words of love
> lead to a life of love.

69

Finishing Touches

John 14:1-6

My Father's house has many rooms; if that
were not so, would I have told you that I am
going there to prepare a place for you?

John 14:2

An elderly Christian woman had entered the final days of her life. Gradually she was succumbing to the cancer that was destroying her body. Her daughter-in-law, also a believer, spent much of her time by her bedside. They talked about many things—the past, the grandchildren, church. As the end approached, they spoke more and more of the Lord Jesus.

In the final hours, the younger woman said something that seemed to comfort the elderly saint. She asked, "What do you think Jesus is doing right now?" After a brief pause, she continued, "I like to think that He is busy getting heaven ready for you. Why, I believe He is putting the finishing touches on your heavenly home right now."

We're not sure what our place in heaven will be like, but we do know this: Jesus went to prepare it for us (John 14:2), and it will be ready when we get there.

As followers of Christ, we can take great comfort in knowing that when we leave this earth we will go to be with the Lord forever. If we have lost a loved one—a spouse, a child, a grandchild—we know that the Lord was aware of her arrival (Psalm 116:15). If we have a loved one ready to go home, or we're nearing that time ourselves, it's reassuring to think that right now Jesus is putting the finishing touches on the place He's prepared for us.

How amazing is it that the God of this grand universe cares enough for you to go to prepare a place for you? Imagine how glorious that place will be! Jesus promised you life "to the full" (John 10:10), and you can be filled with gratitude that this means both now and in eternity.

Our dear Creator God, you have thought of everything!
You not only cast this majestic universe into space
and created a comfortable home for us on earth but
you also prepared a forever place for us with you
in heaven. I can never thank you enough.

Contemplation of heaven is not empty thinking;
it is a clear indicator of love and faith in the One
who is preparing a place for us.

70

Age-Old Wisdom

1 Kings 12:1-7, 12-17

Is not wisdom found among the aged? Does
not long life bring understanding?

Job 12:12

A Singapore newspaper published a special report that contained life lessons from eight older citizens. It began: "While aging brings challenges to mind and body, it can also lead to an expansion in other realms. There is an abundance of emotional and social knowledge; qualities which scientists call . . . the wisdom of elders."

Indeed, wise older people have much to say about life. But in the Bible, we meet a newly crowned king who failed to recognize this.

King Solomon had just died, and in 1 Kings 12:3, we read that "the whole assembly of Israel went to Rehoboam" with a petition. They asked the new king to lighten the harsh labor and heavy taxes his father Solomon had demanded of them. In return, they would loyally serve Rehoboam.

At first the young king consulted the elders (v. 6). But he rejected their advice and accepted the foolish counsel of the young men who had grown up with him (v. 8). He made the burden worse! His rashness cost him most of his kingdom.

The counsel that comes with years of experience is vital, especially from those who have walked with God and listened well to His counsel. That's one of the great gifts grandparents can give their grandchildren: wisdom. Spending time with those special children of our children gives us unmatched opportunities to share godly, age-old wisdom with them. What a privilege!

You've accumulated a lifetime of wisdom. Now what can you do with it? There are some very special children who need that wisdom from their parents' parents. One way to express gratitude to God for equipping you through a lifetime is to make special times with your grandchildren to pass along some of your wisdom to them. Car rides. Fishing trips. Mall outings. Ice cream runs. All times to casually share wisdom.

Dear Lord, show me times when it is natural to convey to my grandchildren some of the things you have taught me about life, faith, and family. Give me words that are helpful and not condemning—kind yet strong enough to make a difference.

The experiences of life and faith reward us with great wisdom, which shouldn't be kept hidden.

71

Really Living!

Psalm 128

Blessed are all who fear the Lord, who
walk in obedience to him.

Psalm 128:1–2

The happy family portrayed in Psalm 128 is God's reminder that believers shouldn't despise the joys of earth. We don't have to choose between a happy, godless life and a somber life of dedication to Jesus. The Christian life is full and rich.

When the Lord Jesus lived on earth, He showed us that a person can be obedient to God, exercise perfect self-control, and still be joyful. Though He knew He would soon go through the agony of hell in dying for sinners on a cruel Roman cross, He was vitally interested in things around Him. His parables and illustrations reveal that He must have paused often to look at flowers as they grew, to watch children at play, and to observe people at work. He enjoyed companionship. In fact, His congeniality gave His enemies an excuse to accuse Him of being a glutton and a drunkard. His example teaches us that we can be pure and serious-minded without withdrawing from society and becoming joyless.

The Christian life is not one of boredom. It is not mere existence. It is the only life of real happiness. When we accepted the Lord Jesus as our personal Savior, believing that He died to pay the price for our sin, we were freed from the burden of trying to earn heaven through self-denial and works. And God gave us the Holy Spirit to live in us and enable us

146

to do His will. When we yield to Him, we can be virtuous, sincere, and happy. That's really living!

Would you consider your Christian life boring or exciting? Do you sometimes long for what is offered by a life of worldly living? Reread the writer's words about Jesus—our Savior and example. His life was full, complete—and sinless! He was really living! Thank God for His example, and strive to live "to the full" as John 10:10 suggests.

Lord, thank you for allowing me to have a free, joyful, fulfilling life as I follow the life-giving instructions in your Word. Help me to keep following you daily and not drift over to the empty promises of a life without you.

There's nothing sadder than seeing someone chase the fool's gold of life and end up shattered and empty.

72

Atheism and Rheumatism

Romans 8:18–25

We know that the whole creation has been groaning as in the pains of childbirth right up to the present time.

Romans 8:22

T he lecturer was energetically denouncing what he believed to be some problem philosophies—communism, atheism, and agnosticism. About halfway through his talk, an older woman stood up and suggested, "I agree with everything you said, sir. But while you're at it, why don't you get rid of rheumatism too!"

As we grow older, we become increasingly aware of the deficiencies and weaknesses of our bodies. Aches and pains enter the picture more frequently, and the vigor and vitality of youth begin to fade. The apostle Paul wrote about our physical problems in Romans 8. He said we "groan inwardly as we wait eagerly for . . . the redemption of our bodies" (v. 23). How wonderful, therefore, is the prospect of that day when all tears shall be wiped from our eyes, and "'there will be no more death' or mourning or crying or pain, for the old order of things has passed away" (Revelation 21:4). Thank God, we as believers can look forward to the time when pain and death are forever banished!

Yes, the day is coming when there will be no more "isms" to bother the child of God—politically or physically. In heaven we'll have flawless bodies like that of Christ himself—free from all ailments. We'll know the blessings of the Lord at their best. Christ will rid the world of everything that's bad—from atheism to rheumatism!

The fact that Scripture addresses the realities of your physical ailments can be a source of gratitude. It shows that God knows you well and cares. And He has provided the ultimate cure—the time when He welcomes you home to heaven. In sickness and in good health, you can say "thank you" to your heavenly Father.

Dear Lord, when I pray for friends and relatives (and myself) who are having physical problems, I know you care. Thank you for the hope of answered prayer and the sure hope of perfection in heaven.

God grants us needed strength for now while offering a sure hope for the future.

73

Heavenly People

Luke 24:44–53

Since, then, you have been raised with Christ,
set your hearts on things above, where Christ
is, seated at the right hand of God.

Colossians 3:1

Believers in Jesus are a "heavenly" people. That's what Paul meant when he told the Ephesians that God has "raised us up with Christ and seated us with him in the heavenly realms in Christ Jesus" (Ephesians 2:6). True, now we live on earth, but "our citizenship is in heaven" (Philippians 3:20). We should therefore "set [our] hearts on things above" (Colossians 3:1) and store up treasures in heaven.

A graphic difference between an earthly minded person and a heavenly minded person can be seen in two Middle Eastern tombs. The first is the burial place of King Tut in Egypt. Inside, the walls are covered with precious metal and blue porcelain. The mummy of the king is enclosed in a beautifully inscribed, gold-covered sarcophagus. Although King Tut apparently believed in an afterlife, he thought of it in terms of this world's possessions, which he wanted to take with him. The other tomb, in Israel, is a simple rock-hewn cave believed by many to be Jesus's burial site. Inside there is no gold, no earthly treasure, and no body. Jesus had no reason to store up earthly treasures. His goal was to fulfill all righteousness by doing His Father's will. His was a spiritual kingdom of truth and love.

Are we storing up treasures for earth or for heaven? When this life is over, all we can take with us are spiritual treasures. Everything else stays here. Let's be Christlike in thought, word, and deed so we will live like "heavenly" people.

What an amazing plan! You live this life as God's child, striving to please Him and trusting His Son Jesus as Savior. And as a reward for your faith in Him, you are rewarded forever. You leave your "stuff" behind and enjoy what God has for you—including basking in His presence. That's heavenly!

Dear Lord, reviewing what you have done for me makes me want to pray even more urgently for the salvation of my grandchildren. I can't take my earthly goods to heaven, but I sure want my family to be there!

The only "things" on earth you can "take with you" to heaven are those who accept and follow Jesus.

74

Heaven without Jesus?

Revelation 22:1–5

They will see his face, and his name will be on their foreheads.

Revelation 22:4

When hymn writer John W. Peterson (1921–2006) first started writing gospel melodies and lyrics, some were rejected by publishers. One such occurrence was especially disturbing. Peterson had just written "Over the Sunset Mountains" after meditating on that glorious day when we will enter the joys of heaven and see the Savior. The music editor he approached seemed pleased with his song but made this small suggestion: "Take out the name Jesus, and enlarge a little more on heaven." Peterson thought, *Heaven without Jesus? That is unthinkable!* So he picked up his manuscript and left.

Soon another song came into his mind that expressed his heartfelt reaction. He titled it simply, "My Song," and it expressed his belief that he had no other song in life to sing but Jesus himself.

God honored John Peterson for not compromising the truth. Eventually both songs were published, and over the years they have brought comfort to many.

As a Christian, Peterson couldn't think of heaven without Christ. He knew that when believers are facing death, they are comforted in the knowledge that joy awaits them in the presence of their Lord.

For the devout follower of Jesus, it's not just heaven that we can't think of without thinking of our Savior. It is life itself as well. His presence gives us hope, courage, and strength—both for today and forever.

What song brings you close to the Lord and reminds you that He is the essence of your existence—the reality that gives you hope? Can you imagine that song without Jesus being involved? Godly music can bring joy to your heart and gratitude to your mouth.

Dear Lord, thank you that someone told me about
Jesus. I cannot imagine my life without Him.
Thank you for sending Him to earth on my behalf.
Help me to continue to sing praises to you.

Jesus. It's the only name we can't live without.

75

Pulled in
Two Directions

Philippians 1:19-26

For to me, to live is Christ and to die is gain.

Philippians 1:21

As Christians, we all want to go to heaven, but we're pulled in two directions because this life also holds great appeal. We're like the girl in Sunday school who listened intently while the teacher told about the wonders of heaven. She concluded by saying, "Everyone who's glad you are going to heaven raise your hands." Every hand shot up immediately—except one. "Why don't you want to go to heaven, Heather?" "Well," she replied, "when I left home, Mom said we were having apple pie for lunch. I love apple pie."

There's nothing wrong with having a strong desire to enjoy life with all its goodness. Marriage, a family, a fulfilling job, travel, recreation—these all have a legitimate pull. However, if the delights of our earthly home are so attractive that we lose sight of God's purpose for putting us here, then we may have to rethink things.

The apostle Paul had mixed feelings too. Although he believed he would be released from prison, he also knew that he could fall victim to Nero's sword. This created a conflict. He longed to be with Christ, for that would be "better by far" (Philippians 1:23) than anything this world held for him. But he also wanted to live—not merely to enjoy life but because he was needed by his fellow believers (Philippians 1:24).

Paul was pulled in two directions, and in both cases it was for the highest reason. It's okay to be pulled in both directions—trusting God for this life and looking forward to the one to come.

That's comforting, isn't it? You don't have to moan because you are still here. And you can enjoy the anticipation of heaven. God's gift of fullness on earth and the sure hope of heaven are reasons to be grateful. What an awesome God!

Lord, thank you for life to the full on earth. You have been so good to me. And at the same time, I look forward to heaven. Help my joy to continue to be full because of your great gifts.

> **God's grace is big enough to allow us two joys:**
> **life on earth and a future in heaven.**

76

"The Face
God Gave Me"

Psalm 139:13–18

I praise you because I am fearfully and wonderfully made.
Psalm 139:14

Many people try to reverse the aging process. Some who are concerned about wrinkles get facelifts, while others have injections to remove unwanted facial lines. Behind this current trend is the notion that an aging face is unacceptable.

But not everyone feels that way. One woman being interviewed about this trend was asked, "Do you like your face?" She responded with conviction, "I love my face! It's the face God gave me, and I accept it happily."

In Psalm 139, David expressed the conviction that his entire being was fashioned by God and therefore is worthy of acceptance. He prayed, "I praise you because I am fearfully and wonderfully made" (v. 14). He also believed that God fashioned all the days of his life (v. 16).

Instead of fighting a losing battle against our waning youthful appearance, we should concentrate on cultivating inner qualities that last forever. One key attribute is an ongoing faith in God, who reassures His people: "Even to your old age and gray hairs . . . I am he who will sustain you" (Isaiah 46:4).

One man once wrote: "Time may wrinkle the skin, but worry, doubt, hate, and the loss of ideals wrinkle the soul." As we gracefully accept the passing of years, God will smooth out the wrinkles of our souls.

Accepting how God made you can give you confidence as you help your grandchildren deal with the many things they might find wrong with themselves. As their great encourager, you can point them to Psalm 139:14 and help them see that there are no mistakes with us as God's creations. You can help them celebrate who they are.

Dear Lord, whenever possible, help me to point out
to my grandchildren how truly special they are in
God's eyes and mine. If they have what they consider
deficiencies in their looks or abilities, help me to be their
biggest cheerleader toward acceptance and confidence.
Help them know the truth of Psalm 139:14.

**Our mirror can't see our heart, the true indicator
of our beauty in Christ.**

77

Arriving Late

Matthew 20:12-16

The last will be first, and the first will be last.
Matthew 20:16

Eddie, an outspoken agnostic, spent his entire life of fifty years denying the existence of God. Then he contracted a debilitating disease, and his health slowly deteriorated. As he lay in a hospice house awaiting death, Eddie was visited almost every day by some Christian friends he had known in high school. They told him again of Christ's love. But the closer Eddie came to dying, the more it appeared he was not interested in God.

One Sunday, a pastor stopped by to visit. To everyone's surprise, Eddie prayed with him and asked Jesus for forgiveness and salvation. Two weeks later, he died.

Eddie denied Christ for fifty years and spent just two weeks loving and trusting Him. But because of his genuine faith in Jesus at the end, he will experience forever God's presence, glory, love, majesty, and perfection. Some may argue that this isn't fair. According to Jesus's parable in Matthew 20, though, it's not about fairness. It's about God's goodness and grace (vv. 11–15).

Have you waited such a long time to trust Jesus for salvation that you think it might be too late? Consider the thief on the cross, who put his faith in Jesus just before he died (Luke 23:39–43). Trust Jesus now and receive His gift of eternal life. It's not too late!

Late salvation is as legitimate a reason to praise God as an early faith in Jesus. Examine your heart. Have you truly given your heart to Jesus—repenting of your sins and trusting His work for you on the cross? If not, do so right now. Age is not important. But faith is essential. Trust Him today.

Dear heavenly Father, thank you for sending Jesus Christ to earth to live a life of perfection. Thank you that He willingly went to the cross to pay for my sins. I repent of my sins and ask You to forgive me and accept me as your child on the basis of Jesus's sacrifice. Save me, Lord. Thank you!

Coming to Jesus late is glorious.
Waiting too late is horrible. Choose Jesus now.

78

A FIRM Foundation

Deuteronomy 6:1–9

These commandments that I give you today are to be on your hearts. Impress them on your children. Talk about them when you sit at home and when you walk along the road, when you lie down and when you get up.

Deuteronomy 6:6–7

Before she was two years old, the little girl did something that would make any grandpa proud: She began to recognize cars by make and year. This all started when she and her daddy began spending time together playing with his old collection of toy cars. Daddy would say, "Katie, get the 1957 Chevy," and she would pick it out of the hundreds of tiny cars. And once, while he was reading a Curious George book to her, she climbed down from his lap and ran to get a miniature Rolls Royce—an exact replica of the car pictured in the book.

If a two-year-old child can make such connections, doesn't that show the importance of teaching children the right things early on? We can do this by using what might be called the FIRM principle: Familiarity, Interest, Recognition, and Modeling. This follows Moses's pattern in Deuteronomy 6 of taking every opportunity to teach biblical truths so that children become familiar with them and make them a part of their lives. Using their interests as teaching opportunities, we repeat Bible stories so they become recognizable, while modeling a godly life before them.

Let's give the grandchildren in our lives a FIRM foundation by teaching them about God's love, Christ's salvation, and the importance of godly living.

Think of the FIRM principle the next time your grandchildren are visiting. It is truly a blessing to have even a small role in making the gospel familiar to them, helping them be interested in godly things, assisting them in recognizing God's truth, and modeling a Christlike life.

*Dear Father, thank you for allowing me to have
an influence on my grandchildren. Make our times
together memorable, fun, and God-honoring.*

**We build a FIRM foundation when we teach,
model, and live out our faith.**

79

Gray Power

Joshua 14:6–12

I am still as strong today as the day Moses sent me out; I'm
just as vigorous to go out to battle now as I was then.

Joshua 14:11

Dutch artist Yoni Lefevre created a project called "Gray Power" to
show the vitality of the aging generation in the Netherlands. She
asked local schoolchildren to sketch their grandparents. Lefevre wanted to show an "honest and pure view" of older people, and
she believed children could help supply this. The youngsters' drawings
reflected a fresh and lively perspective of their elders—grandmas and
grandpas were shown playing tennis, gardening, painting, and more!

Caleb, of ancient Israel, was vital into his senior years. As a young
man, he infiltrated the Promised Land before the Israelites conquered
it. Caleb believed God would help his nation defeat the Canaanites, but
the other spies disagreed (Joshua 14:8). Because of Caleb's faith, God
miraculously sustained his life for forty-five years so he might survive
the wilderness wanderings and enter the Promised Land. When it was
finally time to enter Canaan, eighty-five-year-old Caleb said, "I'm just
as vigorous to go out to battle now as I was then" (v. 11). With God's
help, Caleb successfully claimed his share of the land (Numbers 14:24).

God does not forget about us as we grow older. Although our bodies age and we may not be as healthy as in years past, God's Holy Spirit

renews us inwardly each day (2 Corinthians 4:16). He makes it possible for our lives to have significance at every stage and every age.

Think of all the opportunities you still have to make a positive impact on others. Praying. Perhaps giving financial aid. Maybe working in the church and community. Your grandchildren will notice this, and perhaps they'll sense that this is God still working in you.

Dear God, I know that you have work for me to do—
otherwise why would you have given me these years? Help
me to pray more. To look for new ways to encourage others.
Help me to be like Caleb, who just kept on going.

The more seriously we strive to serve the God who sustains, the greater will be each passing year.

80

The Best Fishing Holes

2 Corinthians 12:1–4

[He] was caught up to paradise and heard inexpressible
things, things that no one is permitted to tell.

2 Corinthians 12:4

Gus was a trout fisherman. Weekends usually found him in his little boat on a nearby lake, casting for fish. After he died, his daughter Heidi sent a note to a fishing buddy of his. She told him she had been talking about heaven with her grandkids since Gus went to his home in heaven. Her six-year-old grandson, who also loved to fish, explained what heaven is like and what Great-Grandpa Gus is doing: "It's really beautiful," he mused, "and Jesus is showing Grandpa Gus where the best fishing holes are."

When Paul reported his God-given vision of heaven, words failed him. He said, "I was caught up to paradise and heard things so astounding that they cannot be expressed in words" (2 Corinthians 12:4 NLT). Words cannot convey the facts of heaven—perhaps because we humans are unable to comprehend them.

While we might gain some comfort from knowing more details about heaven, it is not the knowledge of heaven that assures us; it is our knowledge of God himself. Because we know Him and we know how good He is, we can envision heaven in its beauty. And maybe we can even think that Jesus will show us "where the best fishing holes are"—because that's the kind of God He is!

Heaven may be a faraway prospect in our stage of life, but the assurance that God cares for us enough to create it can put a bit of a spring in our step each day.

The metaphorical "best fishing holes" note tells us that God will provide in heaven a place of unimaginable joy. Maybe not fishing, but surely worshiping and whatever else God has for us there will be praiseworthy.

Dear Lord, thank you for the prospect of heaven. I take great comfort in knowing that my redeemed loved ones are already in your presence. And the reality that heaven awaits me often calms my heart about the future.

> **The reality of heaven in the future gives us hope and assurance in God's goodness right now.**

81

Growing Up

Ephesians 4:1–16

From him the whole body . . . grows
and builds itself up in love.

Ephesians 4:16

Watching youngsters play T-ball is entertaining. In this version of baseball, the players often run to the wrong base or don't know what to do with the ball if they happen to catch it (or catch up to it). If we were watching a Major League Baseball game, mistakes such as the ones T-ballers make would not be so funny.

It's all a matter of maturity.

It's okay for young athletes to struggle—not knowing what to do or not getting everything exactly right. They are trying and learning. So we coach them and patiently guide them toward maturity. Then we celebrate their success as later they play with skill as a team.

Something similar happens in the life of those who follow Jesus. Paul pointed out that the church needs people who will "be patient, bearing with one another in love" (Ephesians 4:2). And we need a variety of "coaches" (pastors, teachers, spiritual mentors) to help us all move toward "unity in the faith" as we strive to "become mature" (v. 13).

The goal as we listen to preaching and teaching and enjoy life together in the church is to grow up to maturity in Christ (v. 15). Each of us is on this journey, and we can encourage each other on the road to maturity in Jesus.

What a joy it is if you see your grandchildren move from playing the recorder in fourth grade to mastering the violin in high school. What a change! And similarly, you rejoice when they grow from Sunday school songs to a deep love for Jesus and a desire to serve Him. If you can have a hand in their spiritual "growing up," what a privilege!

Dear Lord, as the children in our family grow in age, help them to grow in spiritual maturity—open to your leading and willing to serve others in our Savior's name. Thank you for your empowering of them through the Holy Spirit.

Mature Christians can be coaches for the young, instructing them toward maturity.

82

Two Portraits

John 16:19–24

Now is your time of grief, but I will see you again and
you will rejoice, and no one will take away your joy.

John 16:22

Clutching two framed photographs, the proud grandmother showed them to friends in the church foyer. The first picture was of her daughter back in her homeland of Burundi. The second was of her grandson, born recently to that daughter. But the daughter wasn't holding her newborn. She had died giving birth to him.

A friend approached and looked at the pictures. Reflexively, she reached up and held that dear grandmother's face in her hands. All she could say through her own tears was, "I know. I know."

And she did know. Two months earlier she had buried a son.

There's something special about the comfort of others who have experienced our pain. They *know*. Just before Jesus's arrest, He warned His disciples, "You will weep and mourn while the world rejoices." But in the next breath He comforted them: "You will grieve, but your grief will turn to joy" (John 16:20). In mere hours, the disciples would be devastated by Jesus's arrest and crucifixion. But their crushing grief soon turned to a joy they could not have imagined when they saw Him alive again.

Isaiah prophesied of the Messiah, "Surely he took up our pain and bore our suffering" (Isaiah 53:4). We have a Savior who doesn't merely know *about* our pain; He lived it. He knows. He cares. One day our grief will be turned into joy.

No one understands grief like one who has suffered it. Jesus took on His shoulders the pain of all our sins—the agony of all unrighteousness. He knows pain. He knows the grief of having His Father forsake Him. You can have deep gratitude that He is your go-to person in your pain. He understands.

Dear Lord Jesus, thank you for suffering for me. And thank you that in your suffering you can empathize with my pain. What a Savior you are!

Jesus doesn't merely know *about* our pain; He lived it.

83

Growing into Giving

2 Corinthians 8:1–9

Freely you have received; freely give.

Matthew 10:8

I got you a present!" the two-year-old grandson shouted excitedly as he pressed a box into his grandfather's hands. "He picked it out all by himself," the man's wife assured him.

Grandpa opened the box to find a Christmas ornament adorned with his grandson's favorite cartoon character. "Can I see it?" the boy asked anxiously. Then he played with "Grandpa's" present for the rest of the evening. As he watched his grandson, Grandpa just smiled.

He smiled because he remembered the gifts he had given loved ones in the past, like the music album he gave his older brother one Christmas when he was in high school—an album he really wanted to listen to (and did). And he realized how years later God was still stretching him and teaching him to give more unselfishly.

Giving is something we grow into. Paul wrote, "But since you excel in everything . . . see that you also excel in this grace of giving" (2 Corinthians 8:7). Grace fills our giving as we understand that all we have is from God, and He has shown us that "it is more blessed to give than to receive" (Acts 20:35).

God generously gave us the most unselfish gift of all: His only Son, who would die on a cross for our sins and be raised to life. Any who receive this ultimate gift are rich beyond measure. As our hearts are focused on Him, our hands open in love to others.

There is a certain joy in giving that often surpasses the joy of receiving. You see this as you watch the absolute thrill of your grandchildren as they open presents on their birthday and on Christmas. So many people need your help, and that just means more joy in the giving.

Lord, help me to be both wise and generous in my giving.
Help me to sense true needs (with the Spirit's help) and
then enable me to have an open hand where needed.

As we grow in the grace of giving, we will automatically grow in the grace of loving others.

84

A Grandmother's Prayer

James 5:16–20

Confess your sins to each other and pray for each
other so that you may be healed. The prayer of a
righteous person is powerful and effective.

James 5:16

K atherine often told the story of how her grandmother influenced
her as a little girl. Often, Katherine got to stay overnight at her
grandma's house. She would recall that before she went to bed, she
and her grandmother would kneel on a cold, hard floor and pray. While she
prayed, Katherine would squirm and daydream through those prayers—
wondering why Grandma had to pray about such a long list of people.

It wasn't until years later that Katherine figured it out. A series of
city-wide evangelistic meetings were to be held in her home city, and
Katherine accepted the job of contacting people to open their homes
for neighborhood prayer times. One woman she called on asked her,
"Do you know who I am?" and told Katherine her name. The woman
then related that she had grown up next door to Katherine's grandmother, who had often told her she was praying for her salvation,
which meant little to her at the time. Later, however, as a mother
of three the woman was asked to teach a Sunday school class. While
preparing the lesson, she realized she was not a Christian. Then she

remembered the neighbor who had prayed for her. It wasn't long until she opened her heart to the Savior.

Who's on your prayer list? While the list may be too long for fidgeting grandchildren, the people we pray for can be influenced greatly by our intercession. Keep praying. You never know whose life can change.

Sometimes you look around for tasks you can do for our Savior. Creating a prayer list and praying through it is not only a gift for others, it can help you remain close to the Lord.

Lord, make my prayers be not just about me and the things that affect me. Help me to have a circle of people I pray for regularly—starting today. May this privilege of prayer bear fruit in the lives of many others.

Some words we say seem to drift away without effect, but the words we pray have eternal value.

85

Kari's Question

John 3:1–21

You must be born again.

John 3:7

Kari knew her grandpa pretty well. She was aware that he had gone to church all his life and that he was a very good man. She was glad that he had lived an admirable, respectable life. Yet she knew that those things couldn't give him eternal life. So one day while she and her eighty-three-year-old grandfather were riding in the car, this high school senior asked, "Grandpa, have you been born again?"

What Kari didn't know was that her grandfather's former secretary had recently been witnessing to him. This made Kari's question another reason for him to consider his spiritual condition.

Soon after Kari's query, her grandfather and her grandmother were listening to a message by Billy Graham on television and prayed to accept Jesus as their Savior. A few weeks later, Kari's grandfather died and was ushered into eternal fellowship with God.

Has anyone asked you Kari's question? If not, here it is: "Have you been born again?" All of us are dead in our sins—until we are given spiritual life through faith in Christ.

Jesus is the only way to eternal life with God. Any other avenue you take is a dead end. Take time today to consider Kari's question.

It is possible to go through the motions of Christianity—even reading Christian literature—without truly repenting of your sin and asking Jesus to save you on the basis of His sacrificial death, burial, and resurrection. Could that be possible for you? If so, trust Jesus, and you will be eternally grateful.

Dear Lord, I have doubts. I am not sure I know you. Please accept my repentance for my sins as I place my total trust in your work for me on the cross to forgive them. Thank you for saving me.

All of life's roads lead somewhere. But only one—
the road to salvation in Jesus—leads to a full life on earth
and eternal joys forever in heaven.

86

For Young and Old

Psalm 119:9–16

Praise be to you, LORD.

Psalm 119:12

Ellie's grandpa was having health problems and hadn't been himself lately. To cheer him up, Ellie visited him to recite a Bible passage she had memorized for a speech contest.

Grandpa knew that she had won, so he wanted to reward her. Opening his Bible to his favorite passage, he hid some money there. When Ellie arrived, she recited her winning entry, Psalm 119:9–16. Then Grandpa gave Ellie the Bible, and she opened it to find the hidden gift—located at Psalm 119. They had both chosen the same passage!

For Ellie and her grandpa, God's direction led them to a portion of Scripture of vital importance for both young and old. It details how to stay pure in a world of impurity (Psalm 119:9)—something all young people need to do. It explains the importance of hiding God's Word in our hearts (v. 11)—something many older believers depend on as life becomes more difficult. The verses also remind us to praise God, value His standards, meditate on Scripture, and delight in His teachings (vv. 13–16).

Sometimes God surprises us with the way He speaks to us through His Word. He can even use an amazing grandfather-grandchild "coincidence" to put them, and us, face-to-face with some of His most precious promises.

Those moments when grandparents and their grandkids share a love for Scripture are a source of joy. This can be initiated in small, unobtrusive ways. Maybe even verses on the wall or a text to a teen's phone. Look for ways to counter worldly philosophies with God-inspired truth from Scripture. Someday the kids will thank you.

Dear Lord, thank you for your Word, which sustains me, gives me hope, and offers me the glorious salvation available through Jesus. Help me to show my grandchildren how vital the Bible is to them.

The adventure of sharing Jesus with grandchildren has surprises and joys that no other shared experience can bring.

87

Just Go Shopping?

Matthew 16:24–28

Whoever wants to save their life will lose it, but
whoever loses their life for me will find it.

Matthew 16:25

After working for forty years as a teacher, Jane Hanson retired. She and her husband were looking forward to the arrival of their first grandchild.

Retirement is that time of life when many people simply relax, travel, or enjoy hobbies. But Jane heard about a ministry to at-risk youth in a city near her home, and she knew she had to get involved. "I realized there are kids just waiting, and I could make a difference," she said. She began teaching English to a young Liberian man who had been forced to flee his home country because of civil war. Though he was in a safe environment, he didn't understand the new language. Of this ministry opportunity, Jane said with a smile, "I could just go shopping to stay busy, but what fun would that be?"

Jane is making a difference. Perhaps she has learned a little of what Jesus meant when He said, "Whoever wants to save their life will lose it, but whoever loses their life for me will find it" (Matthew 16:25). Giving ourselves to the Lord through helping others takes self-denial, yet one day Jesus will reward that effort (v. 27).

Let's follow Jane's example of love for God and others—no matter what our stage of life may be.

There's a multitude of hobbies that are harmless and even restorative. Even shopping. But if you use all of your free time solving one-thousand-piece jigsaw puzzles, perfecting your lawn, or playing word games, who will teach people a new language, help struggling new moms, and feed people at homeless shelters? Retired or still working, you can find one thing that helps others and says "Thank you" to God for His goodness.

Dear Lord, I don't often think about losing my life for others—I'm more into preserving it for myself. Help me to carve out time to lend a hand to those who are down. Guide me to an area of service where I might even be able to include my older grandchildren.

"Help Wanted" signs are not just for fast-food restaurants and coffee shops; if you keep your eyes and ears open, you'll see signs for help all around you.

88

Leaving It All Behind

2 Chronicles 35:20–27

Jeremiah composed laments for Josiah, and to this day all the male and female singers commemorate Josiah in the laments.

2 Chronicles 35:25

We can learn life lessons even in a comic strip. Upon being told that someone in the community had died, one person in a comic asked, "What did he leave behind?" The other grimly replied, "Everything!"

That's a needed reminder. Think about all those things we've worked so hard to accumulate. Maybe it's a collection of vinyl records of our favorite oldies bands. Or perhaps we have twenty quilts we've painstakingly fashioned. Our house. Our money. It'll all be left to others, and even any "fame" we've achieved—first place in the county fair pie-baking contest—will be soon forgotten.

But there is something we'll leave behind that has a far-reaching significance: our influence—for good or for evil. Especially our family influence.

A godly heritage can remain as the fruit of our earthly sojourn long after we are gone. The Israelites who lamented the death of King Josiah spoke of his noble deeds. And years later, when 2 Chronicles was being written, many people were still recalling his life with joy and praise because he had exerted such a cleansing and uplifting spiritual influence in the nation during his reign.

There is nothing wrong with making wise money decisions and even leaving an impact on a community. But mostly, we should develop a Christlike character that will continue to be an influence for good among those who remain.

Let's pray that when the day comes that we leave everything behind, a godly heritage will be at the top of the list.

As grateful as you are for any wealth you've accumulated or any influence you've left, your greatest reason to thank God is for anything you've said or done that will live on for His glory. It's especially important that your children and grandchildren know of your love for Jesus and your service for Him.

Dear Lord, I pray that when the day comes when I am no longer here, my family will value my influence for you much more than they value what is left behind for my estate sale. Help me right now to leave a godly heritage with every life I touch.

Even a well-written will cannot list all of the key elements of our lives that we can leave behind.

89

Legacy of Affliction

Psalm 119:65–80

It was good for me to be afflicted so
that I might learn your decrees.

Psalm 119:71

ieutenant Paul Galanti, a US Navy pilot, spent six and a half years
as a prisoner of war in North Vietnam. The experience gave him
a heightened sense of ordinary advantages that most of us take for
granted. Speaking of his life in the years after he was released, Galanti
said, "There's no such thing as a bad day when there's a doorknob on the
inside of the door."

After 2,300 straight days in a locked cell, it's easy to see how he con-
siders the privilege of walking outside whenever you please to be one of
life's greatest luxuries.

The writer of Psalm 119 makes a startling statement, "It was good
for me to be afflicted so that I might learn your decrees" (v. 71). From a
time of suffering, he gained a greater love for God and an increased appreciation for His commands. "Before I was afflicted I went astray, but
now I obey your word" (v. 67).

Perhaps you can identify with the words of the psalmist. You've "been
there" and you know what he means. Or you may be in the middle of a
great hardship today. When the days are dark and relief is out of sight,
we need to cling to what we know to be true about the goodness and

faithfulness of God. And then, when He brings us out into the light, we too will see the results and thank God for the legacy of affliction.

Tough words to take: "It is good for me to be afflicted." Consider some circumstances you've lived through in which you came out on the other side saying, "I can see the good in that." Now consider talking to your grandchildren about those times—for they will face trouble in their lives and perhaps need your influential assistance. Can they see in you a gratitude for troubling times?

Lord, you know what I'm going through, and it doesn't look good. Help me to understand what the psalmist meant. Help me to stand strong in trial and seek the goodness in it that you have for me.

Struggling through the darkness of trial is bearable when we know the Light of the World.

90

Feeling Dusty

Psalm 103:13–19

For he knows how we are formed, he
remembers that we are dust.

Psalm 103:14

When Warren mentioned during a weekly ministry team meeting that he was "feeling dusty," his pastor sensed that this was his way of speaking of the physical challenges associated with aging and ill-health. For Warren and his wife, both in their older years, the year had included doctors' visits, surgical procedures, and the rearranging of their home to accommodate in-home care. They were on the other side of the prime of life, and they were feeling it.

One doesn't have to live long before sensing our inadequacies, imperfections, and weaknesses—physically, intellectually, emotionally, and spiritually. God, in the person of His Son Jesus, stepped into our fallen world and cares for those who experience the liabilities of human existence (Psalm 103:13). Furthermore, David wrote, "He knows how we are formed, he remembers that we are dust" (v. 14). The term *dust* takes us back to Genesis: "Then the LORD God formed a man from the dust of the ground and breathed into his nostrils the breath of life, and the man became a living being" (2:7).

Are you feeling a bit "dusty" these days? Welcome to the realities of earthly living for young and old alike. Remember, though, that when we feel most vulnerable, we're not alone. Our compassionate God "knows" and "remembers." He demonstrated His love by sending His Son to provide forgiveness for people like you and me. Even while "dusty," we can trust in Him.

Some people keep their vibrance late into life, but for others, the physical strains of life can show up early. When the body starts to slow down or break down, you have a choice: Live in a world of "woe is me" or trust that "God's got this." He knows. He cares. And He created you in your own special condition. It's tough when things aren't perfect, but praise is a better response than complaining.

Dear Father, you created me just the way you wanted me to be. Please help me to see your hand even in physical ailments. Help me to be a witness of your greatness, even if my body is slowing down.

Feel the presence. Bask in the companionship.
No matter what, follower of Jesus, you are never alone.

91

Answer the Cry

Isaiah 30:15–22

[The Lord] will be very gracious to
you at the sound of your cry.

Isaiah 30:19 NKJV

A grandfather recalls a funny story about a time when his grandkids went to see a stage production of *The Lion King*. Simba
stood over his father, King Mufasa, who had been killed by his
evil uncle. Little Simba, afraid and alone, cried out, "Help, Help, Help!"
At that moment, the man's three-year-old grandson stood on his chair
in the hushed theater and shouted, "Why doesn't somebody help him?"

The Old Testament contains many accounts of God's people crying
out for help. Although their trouble was often self-imposed due to their
waywardness, God was still eager to come to their aid.

The prophet Isaiah had to deliver a lot of bad news, but in the midst
of it he assured the people that "the LORD longs to be gracious to you;
therefore he will rise up to show you compassion. . . . How gracious he
will be when you cry for help!" (Isaiah 30:18–19). Yet God often looked
to His own people to be the answer to that cry for help (see Isaiah 58:10).

Often members of our family need someone to take action to help
them. It is a high privilege to become the hands of God as we respond
on His behalf to cries for help.

What a privilege you have if you can provide help and guidance for grandchildren. You may be able to teach them about a sport they love or help them with schoolwork or remind them of Jesus's love. God's care for them sometimes comes in your willingness to influence their lives.

Dear Lord, as I pray for my grandchildren, help me
to know that I might even be the answer to some
of my prayers. Help me to know when I should be
involved in their lives and to what extent.

When we hear cries for help, it is our hands, directed by our Lord, that can reach out and touch the hurting.

92

The Closet of Prayer

Matthew 6:1-8

> But when you pray, go into your room, close the door
> and pray to your Father, who is unseen. Then your Father,
> who sees what is done in secret, will reward you.

Matthew 6:6

When the Lord Jesus instructed His disciples about prayer in the Sermon on the Mount, He warned them against a public show of piety. Unlike the hypocrites, who stood on street corners and in synagogues where all could see them, the disciples were to find a solitary place to communicate with their Father in heaven.

A fuller meaning of Christ's words came to some tourists who were visiting Abbotsford, the home of Scottish author Sir Walter Scott, near Edinburgh. After the guide had shown them the great author's elaborate, richly furnished study and private desk with its secret compartments, he led the visitors to a door in the corner. It opened into a tiny undecorated room with space only for a table and two benches. The guide said in hushed tones, "This is where all intimately personal and important matters were discussed. When publishers, bankers, or royalty came to talk, they were taken to this room. We Scots call it the 'closet.' You know, like the Bible says in Matthew 6:6."

Prayer is an intensely personal matter between God and us. It's the time when we confess our sins, express our praise, and pour out our hearts to the One who loves us and is deeply concerned about our every need. Important spiritual transactions take place. Promises are made. Victories are won for God.

That's why we need a regular time of quiet prayer. A time to follow the Lord Jesus's command to "go into your room" daily for honest and private conversation with God. Our heavenly Father is waiting.

What a challenge! Setting aside a special time *and* a special place to talk with God. Is that possible? Imagine what it would be like to have an appointment with Him each day to discuss what is on your heart—and to thank Him!

> *Dear Lord, help me not to just talk to you in prayer*
> *but also to hear from you as you lead me to biblical*
> *truths that can help me grow in my faith.*

> **No room in a house can be as important**
> **as the prayer closet—no matter where it is located.**

93

The Stones

Joshua 4

> When your children ask . . . , "What are these
> stones?" then you shall let your children know, saying,
> "Israel crossed over this Jordan on dry land."
>
> Joshua 4:21–22 NKJV

Not long ago, our friends had a gathering at their house and invited a group of people who were all music lovers. Kevin and Ilse, who are both gifted musicians, requested that each person or couple bring a rock for a firepit that was often the site for their evening musical jams. But they didn't want just plain ole rocks. They asked that each one be marked with a name or date or event that indicated how or when everyone had become friends.

God felt that the Israelites needed a reminder of an amazing event in their lives. Although the Jordan River had been at flood stage, the Israelites had been able to cross over on dry ground because God had stopped the water from flowing (Joshua 3:13–17). Something similar had happened years before in an escape from Egypt (see Exodus 14:21–31). On this occasion, however, God instructed His people to build a memorial of stones so that in the future when children would ask about the stones, parents could remind them of the mighty hand of God (Joshua 4:23–24).

As God continually cared for the Israelites, He continues to provide for us today. What "stones of remembrance" will you use to remind your children, grandchildren—and even yourself—of the evidence of God's might?

Whether your grandchildren are younger or older, you've experienced many more years of God's faithfulness than they have. What "stones of remembrance" have you collected over a lifetime? Consider how you can help your grandchild begin their own collection. Maybe there's an item in your collection that will get them off to a great start.

Dear Lord, thank you for being my provider, protector, and guide. I have so many stories of your faithfulness. Help me to share these stories with my grandchildren, so they can begin recognizing your faithfulness in their own lives too.

Every life bears marks of God's faithfulness. We only have to stop and look for them.

94

Healing for a Broken Heart

2 Corinthians 1:3-7

Praise be to the God and Father of our Lord Jesus
Christ, the Father of compassion and the God of
all comfort, who comforts us in all our troubles,
so that we can comfort those in any trouble with
the comfort we ourselves receive from God.

2 Corinthians 1:3-4

I n a small town in Georgia, a large sign was painted on the side of a fix-it shop. The sign read: "We can mend everything but a broken heart."

That clever bit of advertising raises a vital question: Is there anything that can mend a broken heart? When unrelenting sadness darkens each day, or when grief overwhelms us, where can we find comfort and help? Can the human wisdom and care of friends, family, or business associates provide the healing we need? As helpful as their encouragement and support may be, we soon discover that the inner ache of our soul is still there.

There is One, however, who does mend broken hearts. He is referred to as "the Father of compassion and the God of all comfort" (2 Corinthians 1:3). In the person of His Son, Jesus, He left heaven's perfect environment to live in this world of heartbreak. And since He was "tempted in every way, just as we are—yet he did not sin," He can "empathize with our weaknesses" (Hebrews 4:15).

If you are facing deep sorrows, start by casting "your cares on the LORD and he will sustain you" (Psalm 55:22). Pour out your sorrows to the "God of all comfort." He can give relief to your aching soul. In His own time, and according to His own wisdom, He will mend your broken heart.

We all experience sorrow in this life. What do you do when grief hits? You can be grateful that your heavenly Father can empathize with you. He is a real, live, caring God. Find others who suffer too, and perhaps in your shared grief you can find additional help.

Lord, my grief is real, and sometimes others don't understand.
Please help me and comfort me. Then help me to use what
I learn from you to help others who are grieving too.

> The only One who can mend a broken heart completely
> is the One who created that heart and is
> the true source of comfort.

95

Easily Distracted

Titus 2:7–8

Flee the evil desires of youth and pursue
righteousness, faith, love and peace, along with
those who call on the Lord out of a pure heart.

2 Timothy 2:22

Her grandfather was concerned. "Pray for her," he requested as he told a friend fearfully that his teenage granddaughter hadn't been coming to church. She had new interests in her life, including a boyfriend and a car. Grandpa feared that she would forget about the faith he had so carefully nurtured in her over the years.

This young woman did return to church and reestablished her interest in the Lord. But many don't. They get distracted and turn away from their walk with God. In their search for the exciting, the new, the "cool," they leave behind what is most important.

So, what can grandparents do? In Titus 2, Paul said that the older men and women are to be examples to the young, who need to be instructed and encouraged in godly living.

But young people have a responsibility too. Paul said, "Flee the evil desires of youth and pursue righteousness, faith, love and peace, along with those who call on the Lord out of a pure heart" (2 Timothy 2:22).

It's a joint effort that grandparents can help with: our instruction and encouragement coupled with the choice young people make to live as

God would have them live. That combination will help to keep them from being easily distracted.

The privilege you have to influence your grandchildren for Jesus is one to be truly thankful for. And that privilege differs from family to family, so it sometimes requires creative approaches—and prayer. The key is to stay connected to them by showing an interest in their activities and lives.

Dear Lord, you know how much I love my grandkids.
Help me to have helpful opportunities to show and
tell them how important you are—and how loving
and serving you can give them a truly happy life.

The eternal value of each young person compels us to never give up on them.

96

Transmitting Truth

Deuteronomy 4:9–14

Teach [God's ways and instructions] to
your children and to their children.

Deuteronomy 4:9

B ecause they couldn't be with their grandchildren in person during the coronavirus pandemic, many grandparents sought new
ways of connecting. A recent survey showed that a great number
of grandparents adopted texting and social media to help maintain their
precious bond with their grandchildren. Some even worshiped together
with their extended families by video call.

One of the most wonderful ways parents and grandparents can influence their children is by passing down the truths of Scripture. In Deuteronomy 4, Moses charged God's people to "not forget the things" they'd
seen about God "or let them fade from [their] heart[s]" (v. 9). Moses
went on to say that sharing these things with their children and their
children's children would enable them to learn to "revere" God (v. 10)
and to live according to His truth in the land He was giving them.

The relationships God gives us with our families and friends are cer-
tainly meant to be enjoyed. By God's design, they're also intended to be
a conduit to convey His wisdom from one generation to another, "training [them] in righteousness" and equipping them for "every good work"
(2 Timothy 3:16–17).

When we share God's truth and work in our lives with the next generation—whether by text, call, video, or in-person conversation—we equip them to see and enjoy His work in their own lives.

What works best for you as you seek to talk about spiritual things with your grandchildren? We can be grateful for the many resources we can use to introduce them to Jesus and the teachings of the Bible.

Dear Father, there are so many things I could talk about with my grandchildren. Help me to make it a priority to tell them about your truth and about the great life they can have if they trust Jesus and live for Him.

Many grandparents have been receivers of spiritual information for many years; now it's time to be transmitters of God's truth.

97

Longing for God

1 John 4:13–16

My heart and my flesh cry out for the living God.
Psalm 84:2

One day a young mother was at her parents' house with her one-year-old son. Grandpa was getting ready to leave the house on an errand, but as soon as he walked out of the room his grandson began to cry. It happened twice, and each time he went back and spent a moment with him. As he headed out the door the third time, his little lip began to quiver again. At that point his daughter said, "Dad, why don't you just take him with you?"

Any grandparent could tell you what happened next. The grandson went along for the ride, just because his grandpa loved him so much.

How good it is to know that the longings of our hearts for God are also met with love. The Bible assures us that we can "know and rely on the love God has for us" (1 John 4:16). God doesn't love us because of anything we have or haven't done. His love isn't based on our worthiness at all, but on His goodness and faithfulness. When the world around us is unloving and unkind, we can rely on God's unchanging love as our source of hope and peace.

Our heavenly Father's heart has gone out to us through the gift of His Son and His Spirit. How comforting is the assurance that God loves us with love that never ends!

What are some ways God has demonstrated His love toward you? You may want to get a huge piece of paper to write all of them down. How grateful you can be for God's unending love for you in both big and small ways.

Dear Lord, like the grandpa in the story, you hear me.
You know I need you. Thank you for being close to me
when things are good and when things are falling apart.
I need you in both situations, and you are there!

Embedded inside the heart of each person
is the need for God; someone we know
may need to be reminded of that.

98

Now She Knows Everybody

Revelation 21:1-7

"He will wipe every tear from their eyes. There will be no more death" or mourning or crying or pain, for the old order of things has passed away.

Revelation 21:4

Heaven is a wonderful place. In that glorious land God will forever banish all suffering, pain, disappointment, and tears—including the distresses of Alzheimer's disease. The victims of that disorder become so forgetful that they fail to recognize friends and family, even their own husband or wife. Once-familiar people seem like strangers.

Pastor Wilbur C. Rooke shared with a friend what his eight-year-old grandson said when he heard that Wilbur's wife, Myrtle, had died after suffering for fifteen years from Alzheimer's. Without hesitation, David exclaimed, "Well, praise the Lord! Grandma's in heaven, and now she knows everybody!"

Wilbur commented, "Little did David know how important his words were, and what they would mean to so many. If you have ever observed loved ones losing their memory, you can relate to how David felt when he exclaimed, 'Now Grandma knows everybody!' Was it any wonder that his words were a great comfort to those of us who cared the most?"

On that day when we shall all be transformed into residents of heaven, the mist of forgetfulness will be banished by the sunlight of remembrance. Long-forgotten names and places will become vivid when "the old order of things has passed away" (Revelation 21:4).

Who do you know who has gone through that glorious transition from knowing very little to knowing Jesus face-to-face? Can you imagine anything better? What are you most grateful for as you think about the prospect of heaven's glories?

Lord, thank you for hope. In this world with its
ongoing problems and persistent political and
personal squabbles, how comforting it is to know
what you have set aside for me in heaven!

Heaven will cure all ills, for its builder
is the Great Physician.

99

In Every Generation

Psalm 100

The LORD is good and his love endures forever; his
faithfulness continues through all generations.

Psalm 100:5

I t may seem surprising when children don't follow their parents' example of faith in God. Equally unexpected is a person with a deep commitment to Christ who emerges from a family where faith was not present. In every generation, each person has a choice.

Samuel was a great man of God who appointed his two sons, Joel and Abijah, as leaders over Israel (1 Samuel 8:1–2). Unlike their father, however, they were corrupt and "turned aside after dishonest gain and accepted bribes and perverted justice" (v. 3). Yet, years later, we find Heman, Joel's son, appointed as a musician in the house of the Lord (1 Chronicles 6:31–33). Heman, Samuel's grandson—along with Asaph, his righthand man and the author of many of the psalms—served the Lord by singing joyful songs (15:16–17).

Even though a person seems indifferent toward the faith that is so precious to his or her parents, God is still at work. Things can change in later years, and seeds of faith may spring to life in generations to come.

No matter what the family situation may be, we know that "the LORD is good and his love endures forever; his faithfulness continues through all generations."

Hope. This passage gives hope to all who are concerned about children and grandchildren who don't yet follow Jesus. You can be grateful that God continues to work in them. You do what you can, and then you pray and trust.

> *Lord, our hearts break for children or grandchildren*
> *who don't know you. We come to you knowing of your*
> *great love for them, and we ask you to break through*
> *into their lives and guide them back to you.*

God's message of love and compassion for all is thousands of years old—and it has only just begun.

100

The Whole Story

Acts 8:26–37

Philip began with that very passage of Scripture
and told him the good news about Jesus.

Acts 8:35

When a five-year-old grandson asked his grandpa, "Why did Jesus die on the cross?" the two of them had a little talk. The grandfather explained to his grandson about sin and about Jesus's willingness to be our sacrifice. Then the boy ran off to play.

A few minutes later, Grandpa overheard him talking to his five-year-old cousin, explaining to her why Jesus died. She replied to him, "But Jesus isn't dead." The boy replied, "Yes. He's dead. Grandpa just told me. He died on the cross."

The grandpa suddenly realized that he hadn't completed the story. So, they had another talk as he explained to his grandson that Jesus also rose from the dead. They went over the story again until he understood that Jesus is alive today, even though He did die for us.

What a reminder that people need to hear the whole gospel! When a man from Ethiopia asked Philip about a portion of Scripture he did not understand, Philip "told him the good news about Jesus" (Acts 8:35).

Here's how to tell others the good news about Jesus: tell them that we are all sinners who need salvation; that the perfect Son of God died to save us; and that He rose from the grave, showing His power over death. Jesus, our Savior, is alive and is offering now to live His life through us.

When someone wants to know about Jesus, let's make sure to tell the whole story!

The story of salvation is simple. And you can be eternally grateful for that. But you must tell the entire story, making sure those who hear you speak about Jesus know what He did for all of us. And you must tell them clearly about the repentance and faith that comes from those who believe.

Dear Lord, the message of salvation is too important to tell incompletely. Help me to be clear when I share the good news with friends and family.

The story of salvation is simple; share it with your children, grandchildren, and others.

CONTRIBUTORS

James Banks
John Blase
Henry Bosch
Dave Branon
Anne Cetas
Poh Fang Chia
Bill Crowder
Dennis DeHaan
Mart DeHaan
Richard DeHaan
Xochitl Dixon
David Egner
Vernon Grounds
Tim Gustafson
CP Hia
Kirsten Holmberg
Arthur Jackson
Cindy Hess Kasper

Julie Ackerman Link
David McCasland
Haddon Robinson
David Roper
Jennifer Benson Schuldt
Joe Stowell
Herb Vander Lugt
Paul Van Gorder
Marvin Williams
Joanie Yoder

To learn more about the writers of *Our Daily Bread*,
visit odb.org/all-authors.

GENERAL EDITOR

Dave Branon retired in 2021 after a forty-year career as a writer and editor with Our Daily Bread Ministries. Dave has written for the *Our Daily Bread* devotional since 1988—more than 1,200 articles. He has also written 20 books, which include *Beyond the Valley: Finding Hope in Life's Losses* and *Lands of the Bible Today*. He and his wife, Sue, live in Grand Rapids, Michigan, and have four children and eight marvelous grandchildren.